WITHDRAWN

INDIVIDUATIONS
The Novel as Dissent

Terry J. Peavler

UNIVERSITY
PRESS OF
AMERICA

Lanham • New York • London

Copyright © 1987 by

University Press of America,® Inc.

4720 Boston Way
Lanham, MD 20706

3 Henrietta Street
London WC2E 8LU England

All rights reserved

Printed in the United States of America

British Cataloging in Publication Information Available

Library of Congress Cataloging-in-Publication Data

Peavler, Terry J., 1942-
   Individuations : the novel as dissent.

   Bibliography: p.
   Includes index.
   1. Fiction—History and criticism.   2. Characters
and characteristics in literature.   I. Title.
PN3383.C4P4   1987   809.3   87-10549
ISBN 0-8191-6441-0 (alk. paper)
ISBN 0-8191-6442-9 (pbk. : alk. paper)

All University Press of America books are produced on acid-free
paper which exceeds the minimum standards set by the National
Historical Publication and Records Commission.

FOR ALAIN RENOIR

ACKNOWLEDGMENTS

I am grateful to the following persons for their advice and encouragement: Wendell V. Harris, Leon F. Lyday, Louis C. Pérez, Martin S. Stabb, and especially, Linda Deniston-Peavler. I am also grateful to the many students whose graduate seminars were the primary testing ground for my ideas and theories.

This project was made possible by a sabbatical leave from The Pennsylvania State University. The Office of Research and Graduate Studies of the College of Liberal Arts provided support for preparation of the manuscript. The assistance of Glen Kreider, William McCane, Thomas Minsker, and Charles Wissinger was invaluable.

TABLE OF CONTENTS

Preface ix

I. Individuation 1

II. Character/Society/Conflict 31

III. Individualism and Individuation 59

IV. The Novel as Dissent 79

V. A Cultural and Historical Overview 103

Conclusion 127

Bibliography 133

Index 147

PREFACE

This study was originally envisioned in the mid-nineteen sixties when I was just beginning graduate study in comparative literature at the University of California. I was at that time almost rabidly formalist; I had cut my teeth on New Criticism and was then being put through the paces of structuralism. I have, since even long before then, been convinced that of the thousands upon thousands of volumes commonly referred to as "novels," a certain percentage, sizable and perhaps even the majority, form a body of works that should be recognized as a genus separate from the whole. The original goal of this study was to demonstrate, using formalist principles, the unique nature of this genus, to prove that indeed it was the true form of the novel, and to trace its historical patterns to the present time, for I was and am certain that the form has never died, nor has it even been seriously ill.

Despite my efforts over some fifteen years to find the proper formalist keys to adequately isolate and define this form, I eventually had to accept that no meaningful progress had been made; that the very "whatness" of the form excluded it from any precise formalist typology. Only then was I able to recognize a peculiar internal dynamic that has been but partially and sporadically recognized by scholars and which has been totally undervalued. This internal dynamic, which became the proper subject of this study, is sociological and psychological in nature, and appears to be relatively immune to formalist analysis despite the fact that structuralism was born in large part of anthropology.

Contemporary formalist theory has shown us a great deal about how and why narrative functions, and even about many narrative "genres" such as the folk tale and the detective story. It has enjoyed at best, however, but meagre success in probing the hows and whys of the novel, primarily because of its inability to come to grips with the complexities of the type of characters we find in such works, a handicap that the leading formalists themselves have begun to admit. "Character" of the nature that concerns us here cannot be reduced to the easily classifiable status of functions as has been the desire of formalist criticism from Aristotle to the present time. Moreover, because such "characters" are so complex, so dynamic, their actions cannot easily be squeezed into plot "types" or macrostructures, as has also been the tendency. Nevertheless, even in the face of the generic complexities of the novel, it is too early for the structuralists to throw in the towel, for while Terence Hawks[1] and others suggest that each novel is totally unique, I would argue that each is but a "parole" and that if we focus on the structural and structuring relationships of forces within the works (the individual, the society, and the dialectical relationship between them), we can, as did Lévi-Strauss in myth, discover a "langue" or deep structure that defines the novel form.

The very idea of defining the novel in any limited and limiting way is, of course, in great disfavor. Even Alastair Fowler,[2] who represents a refreshing return to serious and systematic genre studies, throws up his hands when he gets to the novel. He believes, perhaps rightly, that the term is too ingrained to be restricted, and so begs the question, discussing subgenres instead of the novel proper as a repertoire of characteristics. The tendency in all theory concerning the novel has been to establish a vast number of categorical possibilities for character, plot, style, technique, etc. and to keep the theory as loose and vague as possible so as to insure its capacity to embrace whatever new work of prose fiction that might yet come along. Raymond Williams emphatically states the majority position: "Great harm is done to the tradition of fiction, and to the necessary critical discussion of it, if "the novel" is equated with any one kind of prose work."[3]

One might argue profitably, however, as does Fowler, that a genre has a minimum repertoire of characteristics, the combined presence of which define it. That a single work may participate in more than one genre need not be of major concern, for the proper purpose of generic identification is not to classify but to understand. One might also argue that genres thus conceived do not change--they may disappear and reappear, but they do not evolve. Nor should the terms used to describe them expand to embrace totally new forms that appear, even if these new forms evolve out of the old. If literary

---

[1]Terence Hawks, *Structuralism and Semiotics* (Berkeley and Los Angeles: University of California Press, 1977).

[2]Alastair Fowler, *Kinds of Literature: An Introduction to the Theory of Genres and Modes* (Cambridge: Harvard University Press, 1982).

[3]Raymond Williams, *The Long Revolution* (New York: Columbia University Press, 1961), p. 278.

terminology could properly and functionally be so expansive we should have but one term: "literature." Even so, the resistance to restrictive genre theory, especially with regard to the novel, is at present insurmountable. And yet, as Fowler astutely points out, we badly need a "finer discrimination than 'the novel' represents" (p. 52). The present study seeks to make a significant step toward filling that need.

Before any progress is possible, "novel" itself must be replaced, for the term, along with other terms traditionally associated with it-- individualism, bourgeoisie, society, realism--has become of little use. Social psychologist Erich Fromm has provided us with both a term and a concept which strike at the very heart of what was traditionally known as the novel: "individuation."[4] Individuation denotes the process by which man, both as a species and as an individual, becomes a unique personality and learns to relate to and interact with the environment, be it social or natural:

> The process of individuation is one of growing strength and integration of [the child's] individual personality, but it is at the same time a process in which the original identity with others is lost and in which the child becomes more separate from them. This growing separation may result in an isolation that has the quality of desolation and creates intense anxiety and insecurity . . . . (p. 31)

Since the characters of a literary narrative are but an illusion created by words on the work's pages, individuation, as a verb, has been slightly modified here to include the process by which the reader comes to recognize and identify with the character's separation from and interaction with his or her environment. As a noun, individuation denotes those literary narratives in which this process occurs.

This study seeks not to expand or complicate, but to simplify and clarify--to uncover a minimal number of irreducible characteristics that define a particular narrative form, a form that, for want of a better term, will be called individuation, thus leaving "novel" unencumbered by meaningful restrictions. Composed as they are of a

---

[4]Erich Fromm, *Escape from Freedom* (New York: Holt, Rinehart and Winston, 1941).

required combination of basic elements, the nature and coalescing of which are the subjects of this study, individuations are, on the elemental, molecular level, unchanging and unchangeable. Yet on the surface, and it is in their surface structures that genres are most frequently studied, individuations are capable of almost infinite variety. Hence the form has remained vital to this day.

Such language, hinting as it does at a useful understanding of "character," "environment," and suggesting hidden evils such as "meaning" and threatening to arouse outmoded ideas like "realism" from the dead would appear to have sprouted from the mind (if an author still were credited with having responsibility for his language) of an either deranged or hopelessly out of touch individual. There is not sufficient space here to take on the deconstructionists, and if there were, I could add little to the arguments of Graff, Hartman, Goodheart, Felperin and many capable others.[5] Even so, deconstruction would provide an unlikely source for contributions to genre theory, focusing as it does on readings so close to the text that they often seem to disappear on the other side. Genre theory has to look at a much larger frame; it has to blind itself to minor differences and split hairs, particularly when those hairs are split over words, even letters. The deconstructors, particularly Hartman's "boa-deconstructors,"[6] for all their contributions to the study of literature, are working in another vein, perhaps in another mine altogether.

Gerald Graff has argued, against the current of much thought since New Criticism, that "belief," "truth," and "reality" are all concepts that have validity. All texts, even deconstructive ones, refer to things outside themselves. Language may be arbitrary, but it is

---

[5] See especially: Gerald Graff, *Literature Against Itself: Literary Ideas in Modern Society* (Chicago and London: University of Chicago Press, 1979); Geoffrey H. Hartman, *Beyond Formalism: Literary Essays 1958-1970* (New Haven and London: Yale University Press, 1970), and *Saving the Text: Literature/Derrida/Philosophy* (Baltimore and London: The Johns Hopkins University Press, 1981); Eugene Goodheart, *The Skeptic Disposition in Contemporary Criticism* (Princeton: Princeton University Press, 1984); Howard Felperin, *Beyond Deconstruction: The Uses and Abuses of Literary Theory* (Oxford: Clarendon Press, 1985).

[6] Preface to Harold Bloom, Paul de Man, Jaques Derrida, Geoffrey Hartman and J. Hillis Miller, *Deconstruction and Criticism* (New York: The Seabury Press, 1979).

nonetheless referential. And even literature that reflects caos reflects something outside itself. Finally, "literature *has* seemed to many people, not all of them stupid or complacent, to make statements, to contribute to man's understanding of how things really are, not merely how they appear to our consciousness" (*Literature Against Itself*, p. 7).

If there is not room at present for a return to the examination of literature in the "big picture," its forms, its history, its relationship to society, whether or not there is or should be a canon, if the answer is affirmative what should be its nature and how and why should it be changed, then surely we must make room or risk abandoning the coherent study of literature to those who would use it purely for political and ideological purposes. As Ralph Cohen has said, "Classifications are empirical, not logical. They are historical assumptions constructed by authors, audiences, and critics in order to serve communicative and aesthetic purposes."[7] And, as Cohen also observed, "to understand the aims and purposes of genre, to understand beginnings and endings, it is necessary to take the road Derrida has not taken" (p. 206).

There are many possible ways in which to approach the problems of genre, particularly as they relate to the novel. Many of those that have been attempted have yielded little in the way of a coherent, comprehensive view of this protean form. Such is not the case of Bakhtin. When the bulk of this study was written I had not had the opportunity to read *The Dialogic Imagination*.[8] If I had, Bakhtin might have had a dramatic impact, particularly on the first two chapters. However, while we distinguish epic from novel in many similar ways (stasis/dynamism, absolute/relative, etc.) we differ in the importance we place on the individual. Bakhtin's "novel" is far broader than my "individuation"; my "genre" is a sub-form of his. I distinguish individuation from romance and the picaresque to a degree Bakhtin does not. He sees the heroes of Greek romances as individuals and private persons, which they may in some sense be, but they

----

[7] Ralph Cohen, "History and Genre," *New Literary History*, 17.2 (Winter 1986), 210.

[8] M.M. Bakhtin, *The Dialogic Imagination: Four Essays*, trans. Caryl Emerson and Michael Holquist, ed. Michael Holquist (Austin and London: University of Texas Press, 1981).

are not "individuated." I believe our discussions of forms supplement one other, and we cross paths at many points. Consequently, I have not made extensive revisions in light of his insights, for although our approaches are quite different, I believe they are equally valid. That we are so close in our conclusions despite having no connection except for those texts we have read in common is reassuring in light of the disfavor into which genre theory has fallen. The distinctions I have found will, hopefully, encourage a return to serious generic discussion of the novel. Other elements will surely prove to be important as well. Bakhtin's concept of "heteroglossia" in "novels of the Second Line" (p. 375) is particularly promising.

The following arguments are, no doubt, what Felperin would classify for the most part as "contextualist." A serious effort has been made to avoid "textual harassment" (Felperin, p. 331).

CHAPTER ONE

Individuation

One of the more difficult tasks confronting the scholar who would write on the novel or on any of its aspects is the selection and definition of terms. The novel, we are told, has dominated the international literary scene for some two hundred years, and yet it is impossible to find more than a handful of definitions of the phenomenon that are fully compatible. The recent boom in literary theory and criticism seems to have done more to muddle than to clarify terminology. Such confusion is not due to the existing corpus of literary works but to a long-standing reluctance on the part of readers and scholars alike to reserve the term "novel" for a particular type of literature. We urgently need a reconsideration of narrative forms and a fresh approach to their definitions. "Novel," for most critics, means extended prose fiction--all such works as have appeared since the novel was first so called, and, as Bakhtin has observed, "the experts have not managed to isolate a single definitive, stable characteristic . . . ."[1] Thus the term can be applied in retrospect to pre-novel works, and Arthur Heiserman and Thomas Hägg can write studies on the novels of antiquity.[2]

At the heart of the problem lies the fact that the novel is recognized by and identified with its surface structure, at the level of discourse, where it can be most difficult to make distinctions between novel, romance, epic, allegory, picaresque tale, etc. (Bakhtin, however, has made important discriminations at the level of language in *The Dialogic Imagination*). In a recent work on the novel, for example, Austin M. Wright discards consideration of the individual in society and realism, and develops a theory of the genre which would

---

[1] M.M. Bakhtin, *The Dialogic Imagination: Four Essays*, trans. Caryl Emerson and Michael Holquist, ed. Michael Holquist (Austin and London: University of Texas Press, 1981), p. 8.

[2] Arthur Heiserman, *The Novel Before the Novel: Essays and Discussions about the Beginnings of Prose Fiction in the West* (Chicago and London: University of Chicago Press, 1977). Thomas H. Hägg, *The Novel in Antiquity* (Berkeley and Los Angeles: University of California Press, 1983). Both studies deal with essentially the same works.

admit *The Aeneid* if it were in prose.[3] One has to conclude, if one accepts Wright's position, that *The Aeneid* or *The Odyssey* or any epic when translated into prose, as most have been repeatedly, becomes a novel. Such discriminations are hardly helpful to the scholar interested in ferreting out basic narrative differences.

What is needed is an examination of extended narrative that penetrates beneath the obvious surface characteristics--prose, characters, society, chronology, etc.--to focus on the nature of the basic elements that combine to make that particular narrative a member of an immediate family of other narratives, but only a distant cousin of still others. Such a consideration, to be most helpful, must not become obsessed with only one such basic element, but with its combination with others necessary to form the molecular structure of a particular type. Such an approach will avoid the pitfall of viewing isolated elements, such as setting, as genre determining characteristics, as occurs in one contemporary theory which includes as distinct genres, "the Negro novel, the Jewish novel, the Depression novel, the Beat novel, the Campus novel."[4] Such discriminations are interesting, but do little to help us understand what type of narrative the term "novel" represents. Our purpose here is to isolate, define, and study a particular type of novel that has been present throughout the form's history, and which indeed has been the dominant, at one time perhaps even the only recognized form.

Of particular importance in the conceptualization of genres, whether on the part of readers, authors, or critics, is the matter of reader expectation. As Jonathan Culler points out, "Comedy exists by virtue of the fact that to read something as a comedy involves different expectations from reading something as a tragedy or as an epic."[5] The concept of reader expectations is also stressed by E.D. Hirsch,[6] although he shows a strong dislike for any genre theory that

---

[3] Austin M. Wright, *The Formal Principle in the Novel* (Ithaca: Cornell University Press, 1982), p. 83.

[4] Bernard Bergonzi, *The Situation of the Novel* (London: Macmillan Press Ltd., 1979), p. 20.

[5] Jonathan Culler, *A Structuralist Poetics: Structuralism, Linguistics and the Study of Literature* (Ithaca: Cornell University Press, 1975), p. 137.

[6] E.D. Hirsch Jr., *Validity in Interpretation* (New Haven: Yale University Press, 1967).

attempts to classify. Indeed, his definition seems to be such that each sentence of a text is a distinct genre. The alteration of a single word will alter the genre of the sentence. His contention that "The only broad genre concept . . . which is by nature illegitimate is the one which pretends to be a species concept that somehow defines and equates the members it subsumes" (*Validity in Interpretation*, p. 110) renders the whole idea of genre useless. The purpose in classification is purely practical: to delimit the corpus of works under discussion and to do so on the basis of certain shared characteristics that are pertinent to the discussion at hand. These shared characteristics are not the invention of critics but the product of literary and cultural history, and readers are drawn to particular forms because they expect to find displayed therein these characteristics.

The confusion concerning the novel form has come about through disagreement on the part of commentators as to the identity and nature of those shared features. The greatest and most common problem has arisen from a reluctance to exclude any lengthy piece of prose fiction, and in particular to exclude any fiction that the commentator finds pleasing. E.M. Forster's now famous definition is exemplary of the trend:

> Any fictitious prose work over 50,000 words will be a novel for the purposes of these lectures, and if this seems to you unphilosophic will you think of an alternative definition, which will include *The Pilgrim's Progress*, *Marius the Epicurean*, *The Adventures of a Younger Son*, *The Magic Flute*, *The Journal of the Plague*, *Zuleika Dobson*, *Rasselas*, *Ulysses*, and *Green Mansions*, or else give reasons for their exclusion?[7]

Others, of course, might exclude some--perhaps even most--of these works from their ideas of the novel. Clearly we are condemned to severe imprecision when we speak of the form: " . . . all theory of the novel has to be remarkably *loose* theory, and theory about *looseness* . . . ."[8]

---

[7] E.M. Forster, *Aspects of the Novel* (New York: Harcourt, Brace & World, Inc., 1927), p. 6.

[8] Malcolm Bradbury, *Possibilities*: *Essays on the State of the Novel* (London: Oxford University Press, 1973), p. 11.

Even so, when one sits down to read "a novel," one sits down with an elaborate, though perhaps imprecise, set of expectations. One might anticipate that the work may take any of a great variety of forms, offer any or all of a broad spectrum of character types, etc., and will, no doubt, have chosen this specific work because of particular expectations aroused by outside information--familiarity with other works by the author, the blurb or the art on the jacket, a review, the recommendation of an acquaintance, and so forth. It is doubtful that one sits down with the purpose of reading a "fictitious prose work over 50,000 words." It is, however, likely, that one will soon abandon the work if it does not satisfy at least some of his or her anticipations.

If we extract from the vast body of possibilities a central core of features that have always drawn readers to the novel form, and restrict ourselves to the consideration of two major such features, highly individualized and developed character(s) and a realistically drawn, mimetic society, we have an essence that at one time defined the novel itself. These, problematic though they may be, are two of the key ingredients of individuations. The third and final ingredient is simply a natural product of the others: conflict.

The novel, in the traditional sense of the word, was recognized and appreciated for its power of individuation. Historically identified with the nineteenth century and associated with the Industrial Revolution, the petite bourgeoisie, and the rise of individualism, it was in every sense a "genre" as defined by Tzvetan Todorov:

> In every period, a certain number of literary types becomes so familiar to the public that the public uses them as keys (in the musical sense) for the interpretations of works; here the genre becomes, according to an expression of Hans Robert Jauss, a "horizon of expectations." The writer in his turn internalizes this expectation; the genre becomes for him a "model of writing." In other words, the genre is a type that has had a concrete historical existence, that has participated in the literary system of a period.[9]

---

[9]Tzvetan Todorov, *Introduction to Poetics*, trans. Richard Howard (Minneapolis: University of Minnesota Press, 1981), p. 62.

Moreover, this form endures to the present day, although its nature and presence have been obscured by the proliferation of the novel and by the steady and rapid expansion of the term's meaning. With regard to what we might consider "deep structure," however, there is still a sizeable body of such works being produced, read, and widely applauded by critics.

While the concepts of "highly individualized and developed character(s)" and "society" are problematic enough, and will be dealt with at some length in due course, even more pressing is the problem of "realism," another legacy of the traditional novel that requires clarification, despite--perhaps because of--its strong association with the novel form.

Indeed the novel has been so strongly identified with realism that in the twentieth century a bitter struggle has developed between the pro and anti-realists:

> Some critics would require the novel to do justice to reality, to be true to life, to be natural, or real, or intensely alive. Others would cleanse it of impurities, of the inartistic, of the all-too-human. On the one hand, the request is for 'dramatic vividness,' 'conviction,' 'sincerity,' 'genuineness,' 'an air of reality,' 'a full realization of the subject,' 'intensity of illusion'; on the other, for 'dispassionateness,' 'impersonality,' 'poetic purity,' 'pure form.' On the one hand, 'reality to be experienced,' and, on the other, 'form to be contemplated.' A dialectical history of modern criticism could be written in terms of the warfare between those who think of fiction that must above all be real . . . and those who ask that it be pure--even if the search for artistic purity should lead to unreality and a 'dehumanization of art.'[10]

It is reasonable to suspect that in insisting on the purity of such polar opposites, critics are in fact discussing two entirely different types of literature, even separate genres.

---

[10]Wayne C. Booth, *The Rhetoric of Fiction* (Chicago: University of Chicago Press, 1961), pp. 37-38.

It seems only proper to identify the novel through those characteristics that first distinguished it as a new literary form. Realism is surely one of the most central of these, but realism itself has a variety of interpretations, and demands some clarification.[11] Despite Roland Barthes' protestations[12] realism, mimesis, representation, plausibility, and numerous related concepts are vital to the reading and understanding of thousands of narratives. For Barthes, "reality" lies not in what is "natural" but in what is "logical" (*Image-Music-Text*, p. 124), an argument that is not valid for all narratives, for logic does not concern itself with the validity of premises but the tightness of the argument. An argument may be perfectly logical without being verisimilar. Todorov argues most persuasively that verisimilitude is not to be confused with truth in narrative, and indeed truth is dispensable while verisimilitude is not.[13] It does not matter a great deal which of Todorov's meanings for verisimilitude we prefer, or whether we accept the term's full polysemy; at least two meanings are especially relevant to individuations: 1) "verisimilitude is the relation of the specific text to another, generalized text which is called 'common opinion'"; 2) "we speak of a work's verisimilitude insofar as the work tries to convince us it conforms to reality and not to its own laws" (*Poetics of Prose*, p. 82 and p. 83).

Todorov provides an important bridge between the principles of internal logic championed by Genette and Barthes and the realism of individuations. We might add that plausibility or verisimilitude plays off of and depends to a large degree upon reader gullibility. What is plausible for one reader is met by another's skepticism. What is worse, verisimilitude can change as the scientific and philosophic beliefs of a people (i.e. the text of "common opinion") change. Thus a futuristic work of science fiction could, with the passage of time, become plausible, or scientific advancement could render a once plau-

---

[11] For a spirited debate on realism, convention, and verisimilitude with arguments by Margaret Gilbert, Menachem Brinker, and Nelson Goodman, see *New Literary History*, 14.2 (Winter 1983), 225-276. Michel Foucault also makes important observations in his essay, "The Prose of the World," in *The Order of Things: An Archaeology of the Human Sciences* (New York: Pantheon Books, 1970), pp. 17-45.

[12] Roland Barthes, *Image-Music-Text*, trans. Stephen Heath (New York: Hill and Wang, 1977), pp. 123-124.

[13] Tzvetan Todorov, *The Poetics of Prose*, trans. Richard Howard (Ithaca: Cornell University Press, 1977), pp. 80-88.

sible work obsolete. Realism, it would appear, is in the eye of the beholder, to the point that some argue that sheer fantasy is but a form of realism.[14]

Realism, if we take that term to mean what the author imitates, what he or she thinks he or she sees--and hence what the reader believes the work faithfully reveals about the world, may be less problematic than reality. As today we stand on the uncertain ground of quantum physics, any belief about reality or realism requires an act of faith on the part of authors and readers alike. Yet even Einstein was not hesitant to take that step; he believed in causality despite the fact that his scientific theory and research denied it.

Reality may well stand in relation to us as God did to Unamuno: we believe because we have to. Quantum theory and the increasingly accepted cladist theory (the agnostic rejection of evolution) may prove to be "true" but the consequences may be unacceptable in our lives and in those fictions we term "realistic." As Robert Alter argues in refutation of Genette:

> ... it is by no means clear why the choice of details in a fictional narrative cannot be dictated simultaneously by principles of internal coherence and by the writer's sense of a just, plausible correspondence to the social, moral, psychological facts of real existence as he understands them.[15]

One might add that if Barthes is willing to advance the theory that narrative is based on a logical fallacy, *post hoc, ergo propter hoc* (*Image-Music-Text*, p. 94), then we should also accept that a certain type of narrative may legitimately be based on a perceptual fallacy as well, again shared by author and reader.

This, of course, does not solve the problem of "datedness" of some works once thought to be realistic. However, such datedness tends to be a problem only in cases involving an omniscient authorial voice that sees and speaks for itself. In first person narratives and in those

----

[14]See, for example, Paul Coates, *The Realist Fantasy: Fiction and Reality Since Clarissa* (London: Macmillan, 1983), p. 1.

[15]Robert Alter, *Motives for Fiction* (Cambridge and London: Harvard University Press, 1984), p. 9.

third person narratives that confine themselves to the perspective(s) of character(s) within the narrative proper, the problem tends to disappear, for readers can always dismiss the incongruences between the work's portrayal and their own personal perceptions of reality on the grounds that the individuals living at the time and place depicted shared those beliefs.[16] In other words, we tend not to mind if characters believe in werewolves, but we mind very much if God does. Mary McCarthy's insistence on "The Fact in Fiction" loses force quickly if a deranged or superstitious character and not an external narrator observes the flight of Mephistopheles.[17] In the absence of such a perspective, the realism of individuations, like that of the early novel, seeks to convince us of the fidelity of the portrayal to the "facts" of life: "it surely attempts to portray all the varieties of human experience . . . ."[18]

One aspect of reality that has always played a vital role in the novel is the concept of time and its steady flow. As Arnold Hauser points out, "The novel develops its formal principle from the idea of the corrosive effects of time, just as tragedy derives the basis of its form from the idea of the timeless fate which destroys man with one fell blow."[19] If a lengthy period of time should pass without those corrosive effects, we have good reason to be suspicious. That Penelope should weep steadily for twenty years without those tears having a grave effect on her desirability as a woman clearly demonstrates that

----

[16]Mario Vargas Llosa thus gets around the sticky problem of phrenology, which was philosophically vital to Euclydes da Cunha's *Os Sertões*, upon which *Guerra del fin del mundo (War of the End of the World)* was based, by introducing a special character, and along with him his perspective of blind belief in phrenology.

[17]For example, the Cuban novelist, Alejo Carpentier, set one of his earlier novels in Haiti and provided a strong atmosphere of voodoo. When one of his characters, Mackandal, takes physical flight to avoid execution, it is believable in context. Even so, those who claim to have seen the levitation are all active practitioners of voodoo, and the narrator observes that no one noticed when Mackandal was forced back into the flames. See Alejo Carpentier, *The Kingdom of this World (El reino de este mundo)*. For Mary McCarthy's side of the argument, see "The Fact in Fiction," *Partisan Review*, XXVII, 3 (Summer 1960), 438-58.

[18]Ian Watt, *The Rise of the Novel: Studies in Defoe, Richardson and Fielding* (Berkeley and Los Angeles: University of California Press, 1967), p. 11.

[19]Arnold Hauser, *The Social History of Art*, (New York: Alfred A. Knopf, 1952), p. 791.

hers is a world of epic, not novelistic time. The fact that others, including Odysseus, have aged considerably, does not alter the fact that in many ways time is suspended.

Many studies have been devoted to the exploration of time as it relates to the novel, but one of the most valuable insights is offered by Frank Kermode,[20] who, following the leads of Oscar Cullman and John Marsh, makes a distinction between *chronos* and *kairos*. *Chronos* is passing time such as is measured by clocks and calendars, while *kairos* is "a point in time filled with significance, charged with a meaning derived from its relation to the end" (*Sense of an Ending*, p. 47). Seasons, because of their symbolic meaning, are *kairoi*. Hours and days are *chronoi*. *Chronos* is the time required in an individuation. Even though *kairoi* may be used to great artistic advantage, to replace *chronos* with *kairos* as is sometimes done in overtly archetypal narratives, is to pass beyond the limits of individuation.

Coupled with realism, and yet in many ways distinct from it, is character, which poses some of the most difficult yet important keys to individuation. As William John Harvey points out, the consideration of character raises most urgently and comprehensively the adequacy of the novel's relation to life.[21] Harvey's point concerning the novel's relation to life is one of the oldest arguments concerning the nature of the novel. As Henry James believed, "The only reason for the existence of the novel is that it does attempt to represent life."[22] Furthermore, the inextricable nature of character and action is one of the least arguable points James made concerning fiction:

> What is character but the determination of incident? What is incident but the illustration of character? What is either a picture or a novel that is *not* of character? What else do we seek in it and find in it? It is an incident for a woman to stand up with her hand resting on a table and look out at

---

[20]Frank Kermode, *The Sense of an Ending* (New York: Oxford University Press, 1968), p. 47. The studies cited by Kermode are Oscar Cullman, *Christ and Time* and John Marsh, *The Fullness of Time*.

[21]William John Harvey, *Character and the Novel*, (Ithaca: Cornell University Press, 1965), p. 208.

[22]Henry James, *The Art of Fiction and Other Essays* (New York: Oxford University Press), p. 5.

you in a certain way; or if it be not an incident I think it will be hard to say what it is. At the same time it is an expression of character. (*Art of Fiction*, p. 13)

Realism, just as it requires verisimilitude of setting, action, and character, leads to well-developed, interiorized characters. The argument that the psychological novel was not realistic because it was not objective is totally invalid. Characters can be fully developed and revealed equally well by what they do, by what they say, or by what they think. What matters is that they stand or fall as believable imitations of human individuals and that they be subject to the same laws of nature that govern those who write and read about them. While Lukács recognized the novel as a form that pits the interiority of character against the world,[23] the limitation to his argument is that he fails to address the questions of believability or humanness of the character, and of the specificity of the society portrayed. For Lukács it is "the world" writ large, which falls beyond the limits of individuations. Scholes and Kellogg describe the conflict more accurately:

> These great realistic novels generate their power by the tension they exploit between their mimetic and mythic characteristics. The characters are highly individualized versions of recognizable social types, and the patterns through which they move are woven out of the *mythos* of the tragic drama.[24]

To interiorize a character is to endow with individuality, and it is within the conflict between the individual and surrounding circumstances that we find the key to individuations as a distinct narrative genre:

---

[23]Georgy Lukács, *The Theory of the Novel*, trans. Anna Bostock (Cambridge: MIT Press, 1971), p. 70.

[24]Robert Scholes and Robert Kellogg, *The Nature of Narrative* (New York: Oxford University Press), p. 234.

> It is the elusive space of the boundaries between individual and group that the novel has taken as its own, the interface between the potentially utter uniqueness of the myriad contingencies in any single life on the one hand, and on the other, the patterns particular cultures provide for giving cohesion, shape, and meaning to those contingencies--without which they would not even be comprehensible **as** contingencies.[25]

It is the concretization of this collision between "self" and "other" that gives individuation both its form and its power.

Just as to interiorize is to individualize, so too does the process lead to reader understanding and empathy, for when we recognize that even the most despicable traits flow from the human nature of the character, we begin to value its life as if it were human. A shallow or flat character may represent evil in a literary work, but an individualized character may only *be* evil. There are few readers who can rejoice in the death of an Ahab or an Artemio Cruz even though virtue is hardly a trait that marks their lives. It is only through our sympathy with characters as human individuals that the conflict between character and circumstance can derive its power and such conflict is the *sine qua non* of the genre itself.

The mimetic nature of individuations--the close imitation of social and physical setting, the careful development of believable human characters--makes it difficult if not impossible to stay within the limits of the genre and still construct a plot line that illustrates abstract concepts of a moral or aesthetic nature: "The domain of the novel is the individual and his social relationships, and it tends to present its subject less in terms of ethical categories than in terms of chronological and causal sequences."[26] Moreover, the fidelity of novelists to mimetic characterization and action has led either to a constant struggle between character and plot or to the supremacy of the former over the latter: "the importance of the plot is in inverse proportion to that of character" (Watt, *Rise of the Novel*, p. 279). Indeed, Watt goes on

---

[25]Michael Holquist and Walter Reed, "Six Theses on the Novel--and Some Metaphors," *New Literary History*, 11.3 (Spring 1980), 422.

[26]Bernard J. Paris, "Form, Theme, and Imitation in Realistic Fiction," *Novel: A Forum on Fiction*, 1.2 (Winter 1968), 141.

to argue that in the most "typical" novels, those that we have called individuations, the plot attempts only to embody the ordinary processes of life, "thus coming to depend completely on characters and their interrelationships" (p. 280).

Previous to the novel, the bulk of narrative literature sought to portray and preserve the values of society while lyric and some forms of tragedy stood rather alone in defense of the thoughts and emotions of the individual. The early novel brought these two points of view into a collision not to determine the rightness or the wrongness of the opposing sides, but to explore the nature of the conflict itself: "The novel's great virtue lay in finding a way to combine the tragic concern for the individual with the comic concern for society" (Scholes and Kellogg, p. 231). In comparison with earlier forms, the conflict is less concentrated, less spectacular. The sufferings and failings of the characters are, in Frye's terms, more pathetic than tragic: ". . . while tragedy may massacre a whole cast, pathos is usually concentrated on a single character, partly because low mimetic society is more strongly individualized."[27]

Essentially then, individuations imitate human life. The world and the characters they portray are subject to the natural laws that bind us all. Within this man-made universe, governed by the inexorable march of time, human individuals move within and collide with a carefully specified society:

> Words must be composed in such a way that through the activity of reading there will emerge a model of the social world, models of the individual personality, of the relations between the individual and society, and, perhaps most important, of the kind of significance which these aspects of the world can bear. (Culler, p. 189)

Because it has been human nature, at least for the last few centuries, to empathize and sympathize with each human individual in the struggle to defend his or her personal rights and values against the political, social, and religious demands of society--be they physical,

---

[27]Northrop Frye, *Anatomy of Criticism: Four Essays* (New York: Atheneum, 1967), p. 38.

economic or moral--individuations are critical of societies, governments, and religious institutions, and hence represent open threats to the *status quo*. By its inherent nature the form moves the reader to recognize the validity of the perspective of the individual, even when he or she does not fully share that perspective. To write an individuation is to be a dissident voice, and the possibilities for dissidence have controlled the history of the form.

Further evidence of dissension, in this case of a literary sort, has been well documented in studies of the novel as a self-conscious genre,[28] and more recently, Holquist and Reed have called for "a recognition of the dialectical position of novels in the larger system of literary and sociological ideologies: their critique of literature as an institution, their opposition to system as a mode of thought" ("Six Theses," p. 413).

The novel (and hence individuations), paradoxically, is a literary artefact intended for mass production and consumption--indeed made possible by the capabilities of mass production and consumption--yet it is produced by a solitary individual to be read by a mass of solitary individuals and it has the solitary individual as its subject. Each novel is, or seeks to be, novel:

> The novelist has isolated himself. The birthplace of the novel is the solitary individual, who is no longer able to express himself by giving examples of his most important concerns, is himself uncounseled, and cannot counsel others. To write a novel means to carry the incommensurable to extremes in the representation of human life. In the midst of life's fullness, the novel gives evidence of the profound perplexity of the living.[29]

---

[28] See especially Robert Alter, *Partial Magic: The Novel as a Self-Conscious Genre* (Berkeley and Los Angeles: University of California Press, 1975) and Walter L. Reed, "The Problem with a Poetics of the Novel," *Novel: A Forum on Fiction*, IX, 2 (Winter 1976), 101-113.

[29] Walter Benjamin, "The Storyteller: Reflections on the Works of Nikolai Leskov," in *Illuminations*, trans. Harry Zohn, ed. Hannah Arendt (New York: Harcourt, Brace & World, Inc., 1968), p. 87.

With these unique aspects of individuations in focus, we can distinguish them from other novelistic forms. A major and immediate distinction can be drawn in terms of external control over content. An author who constantly holds his characters in line to insure that the proper forces emerge victorious in the end and that the correct values are upheld is not writing an individuation. It is one thing to portray social, or national, or moral, or aesthetic values, but quite another to insist that they control the action. A primary difference between epic and individuation is that in the former the individual must always be subservient to and if necessary sacrificed for the national good, while in the latter, even though the individual may be sacrificed, the reader sides with him or her to the bitter end. Romance, like epic, is governed by values other than those which may be upheld in the daily lives of personalized, individualized human beings. Control need not, indeed cannot, be totally absent from an individuation, but once the characters have been created and endowed with their own unique personalities and the social setting within which they move has been established, the characters must find their own ways through the maze of life. As Todorov has shown, such narratives hold forth the possibility of a variety of developments, based on the characters' abilities to choose. In older narrative forms, there was no choice. (*Poetics of Prose*, p. 68).

While the purpose here is not to develop a full theory of genres, it is important to distinguish individuations from other major narrative forms, in particular the epic, the romance, and the picaresque tale. Epic takes place in an ideal, frozen time (*kairos*) and it embodies ideal, frozen values: "In the epic, the preservation of an ordered society is the highest good" (Scholes and Kellogg, p. 36). The world of individuations, in contrast, is in a constant state of flux: " . . . we can hardly deny that the explosion of the fixed hierarchy of values and its replacement by the dynamism of a constantly changing order of values is also an aspect of the increased emancipatory content of the novel as compared with the epic . . . ."[30] The reasons for this literary change, as we shall see in a later chapter, are inextricably tied to cultural history. The epic world is one of clarity: its society is ordered and simple, its values clear and constant, its characters shallow and symbolic. The epic world is beautifully self-contained: "this 'real'

---

[30] Ferenc Fehér, "Is the Novel Problematic? A Contribution to the Theory of the Novel," *Telos*, 15 (1973), 62.

world into which we are lured, exists for itself, contains nothing but itself . . . ."[31]

The early novel offered reality in opposition to this ideal world. And in addition to physical reality, it put forward seemingly real individuals as characters--individuals who were far freer than epic heroes: "*Don Quixote* is the first *novel*, because its hero possesses a freedom which is in principle unthinkable in the epic: the ability to revolt in the very midst of real experience and to oppose to it a different, merely possible experience" (Fehér, p. 51). Ortega y Gasset makes a similar distinction between epic and novel characters:

> If the epic figures are invented, if they are unique and incomparable natures, which in themselves have poetic value, the characters of the novel are typical and nonpoetic; they are taken, not from the myth . . . but from the street, from the physical world, from the living environment of the author and the reader.[32]

Perhaps no scholar has written more about the nature of character in the epic and the novel than has Lukács, yet nowhere do the issues seem to become so murky as in his writings. Much of the confusion stems from his failure to recognize that on a deep, elemental level, many modern day novels are based on the same principles of character, setting, and conflict as the epic, while others continue the tradition of individuation. This failure leads him to vacillate between insisting that the novel, is not just an outgrowth from the epic, but also a continuation of it, and concluding that the two forms are vastly different:

> The epic and the novel, these two major forms of great epic literature, differ from one another not by their authors' fundamental intentions but by the given historico-philosophical realities with which the authors were confronted. The novel is the epic of an age in which the extensive totality of life is

----

[31] Erich Auerbach, *Mimesis*: *The Representation of Reality in Western Literature*, trans. Willard R. Trask (Princeton: Princeton University Press, 1968), p. 13.

[32] José Ortega y Gasset, *Meditations on Quixote*, trans. Evelyn Rugg and Diego Marín (New York: W.W. Norton & Company, Inc.), p. 127.

no longer directly given . . . (*Theory of the Novel*, p. 56)

Yet in another context he argues: "The novel tells of the adventure of interiority; the content of the novel is the story of the soul that goes to find itself . . . . the epic world excludes adventure in this essential sense . . ." (p. 89).

Further, Lukács has difficulty with the precise meaning of "individual." In *The Historical Novel* he argues that "The heroes of the epic are, as Hegel says, 'total individuals who magnificently concentrate within themselves what is otherwise dispersed in the national character, and in this they remain great, free and novel human characters.'"[33] In *The Theory of the Novel*, however, he states that: " . . . one of the essential characteristics of the epic is the fact that its theme is not a personal destiny but the destiny of a community . . ." (p. 66). The issue here, then, seems to become one of interiority, of personality. Yet in another portion of the same work, Lukács argues that the hero of a novel is merely an instrument: "The epic individual owed his significance to the grace accorded him, not to his pure individuality. But just because the novel can only comprise the individual in this way, he becomes a mere instrument . . ." (p. 83).

The contradictory and confused nature of Lukács' arguments is due to his conviction that the novel is purely a continuation of the epic, and his failure to recognize the difference between individuations and, for example, the works of Scott, which on a basic level are epic in nature. It is much more profitable to distinguish between these superficially similar narrative forms in terms of the degree of individuality of the characters and the nature and resolution of the conflict between individual desires and needs and the communal good. As Clayton Meeker Hamilton points out:

> The characters in the great epics are memorable mainly because of the part that they play in advancing or retarding the victory of the vast and social cause which is the subject of the story. Their virtues and their faults are communal and representative: they are not adjudged as individuals, apart from the conflict in which they figure: and as a conse-

---

[33] Georgy Lukács, *The Historical Novel*, trans. Hannah and Stanley Mitchell (London: Merlin Press, 1962), p. 36.

quence, they are rarely interesting in their individual traits. It is in rendering the more intimate and personal phases of human character that epic literature shows itself, when compared with the modern novel, inefficient. The epic author exhibits little sympathy for any individual who struggles against the cause that is to be established.[34]

From this perspective, it becomes clear that a great many novels are primarily epic in nature. Far too much importance has been given the use of heroic verse, the intervention of the gods, and other major and minor epic conventions. The works of Scott tend to be either epics or romances, as do the bulk of prose fiction works that appear in emerging nations during their formative years when the trend is to promote national causes. Most Spanish American fiction up to Mariano Azuela's *Los de abajo* (1915) and even after clearly shows this epic nature. The works discussed by Susanne Howe in *Novels of Empire*[35] are also epics for they too exist to show the nobility of national causes. And finally, post-revolutionary fiction of recent years, particularly in those countries where socialist governments have emerged victorious, is epic, because but for rare exceptions, it insists on the need for the individual to be sacrificed to the national good. The dissidence so central to individuations cannot be, or is not tolerated.

Odysseus returns home not out of any strong personal commitment, for he finds enough attractions to keep him away forever, but because he must. As Paul Goodman points out, "The exploit must be done because it is necessary. The hero must perform it because he can, he has the requisite virtue; and it is his task, otherwise he is not acting out his habit."[36] Aeneas may be an epic hero, but Dido, who is disposed to place her personal needs above the needs of her nation, is

----

[34]Clayton Meeker Hamilton, *The Art of Fiction: A Formulation of its Fundamental Principles* (New York: Doubleday, Doran & Company, Inc., 1939), p. 220. This work has been almost totally ignored, yet is one of the finest studies ever done on the novel form.

[35]Susanne Howe, *Novels of Empire* (New York: Columbia University Press, 1949).

[36]Paul Goodman, *The Structure of Literature* (Chicago: The University of Chicago Press, 1959), p. 68.

a perfect heroine for an individuation. Or, as Todorov would argue, epic is in the obligative, individuation in the optative mood (*Poetics of Prose*, p. 144). If we read the *Aeneid* as a history of Aeneas' conflict between *furor* and *pietas*, we may conclude that, contrary to the normal, historical interpretation, the *Aeneid* is an anti-epic because the final view we have of the hero is one in which *furor* is totally victorious as the enraged Aeneas slays Turnus. Even so, this reading can be used only to demonstrate the anti-epic nature of the work. It is still far from being an individuation. Epic heroes may be both flawed and frail, but this does not suffice to make them the individuals that characterize individuations nor does it alter the nature or the outcome of the internal conflict that distinguishes the two types of narrative: "In general, since the performance of the exploit is important because of the group rather than the person, the man may be destroyed by his frailty, like Roland, and yet the group be saved by virtue of its representative" (Goodman, p. 70).

Romance, like epic, is populated by idealized types. Again, characters rich in symbolic value move through a series of actions of great importance that highlight the virtues and flaws of the actors. As early as 1785 Clara Reeve made a clear distinction between novel and romance:

> The Romance is an heroic fable, which treats of fabulous persons and things.--The Novel is a picture of real life and manners, and of the times in which it is written. The Romance in lofty and elevated language, describes what never happened nor is likely to happen.--The Novel gives a familiar relation of such things, as pass every day before our eyes, such as may happen to our friend, or to ourselves . . . .[37]

William Gilmore Simms, like Hawthorne, insisted on the distinction between romance and novel: "You will note that I call 'The Yemassee' a romance, and not a novel. You will permit me to insist upon that distinction. I am unwilling that the story shall be examined by any other than those standards which have governed me in

---

[37] Clara Reeve, *The Progress of Romance and the History of Charoba, Queen of Aegypt* (New York: The Facsimile Text Society, 1930), p. 111.

its composition...."[38] Simms rightly views the romance as a form that has far more in common with the epic than with the traditional novel:

> The standards of the Romance... are very much those of the epic. It invests individuals with an absorbing interest--it hurries them rapidly through crowding and exacting events, in a narrow space of time--it requires the same unities of plan, of purpose, and harmony of parts, and it seeks for its adventures among the wild and wonderful. It does not confine itself to what is known, or even what is probable." (*The Yemassee*, p. 6)

Simms also recognizes that the reader who confuses the two forms will be disappointed in his reading:

> It [the romance] differs much more seriously from the English novel than it does from the epic and the drama, because the difference is one of material, even more than of fabrication. The reader who, reading Ivanhoe, keeps Richardson and Fielding beside him, will be at fault in every step of his progress. (p. 5)

Scholes and Kellogg make an important distinction between "illustrative" and "representational" characters. This distinction is one of the most valuable ones we can make in separating individuation from epic and romance. The characters, at least the major ones of individuations, are representational; those of romance, illustrative:

> Illustration differs from representation in narrative art in that it does not seek to reproduce actuality but to present selected aspects of the actual, essences referable for their meaning not to historical, psychological, or sociological truth but to ethical and metaphysical truth. (*Nature of Narrative*, p. 88)

---

[38] William Gilmore Simms, Prefatory Note to *The Yemasse* (New York: American Book Company, 1937), p. 4.

Northrop Frye makes a similar distinction: "The romancer does not attempt to create 'real people' so much as stylized figures which expand into psychological archetypes," and later: "the novelist is freer to enter his characters' minds because he is more objective" (*Anatomy of Criticism*, pp. 304 and 308). This is not to say that the characters of a novel may not have symbolic or illustrative value. Many novels, including individuations, are crowded with symbolic figures, and often even main characters illustrate, at least in the early stages of the narrative, certain values or concepts. In individuations, however, these values are subject to the same scrutiny and vicissitudes as the characters in which they reside. Flaubert, when he says "Madame Bovary c'est moi"[39] does not mean that Emma Bovary represents him in a tightly controlled symbolic way, but that her conflict between idealism and pragmatism, or romanticism and realism, parallels his. To use the terms of the Mario Vargas Llosa,[40] Flaubert is "exorcising his demons" by giving them a literary form and then allowing the conflict to work itself out to a conclusion.

Just as the characters of romance, when compared to those of individuations, are less realistically drawn, so too is the world they inhabit less mimetic:

> The romance, following distantly the medieval example, feels free to render reality in less volume and detail. It tends to prefer action to character, and action will be freer in a romance than in a novel, encountering as it were, less resistance from reality.... Being less committed to the immediate rendition of reality than the novel, the romance will more freely veer toward mythic, allegorical, and symbolistic forms.[41]

----

[39] Gustav Flaubert. This statement is attributed to Flaubert by many commentators and there is little reason to doubt its authenticity. I have not, however, succeeded in tracing it back to an original source.

[40] Mario Vargas Llosa, *García Márquez: Historia de un deicidio* (Barcelona: Barral Editores, S.A., 1971).

[41] Richard Chase, *The American Novel and Its Tradition* (Garden City: Doubleday & Company, Inc., 1957), p. 13.

This idealization of both the world and the characters presented tends to affect even the language in which the work is written: "... monologues tend to be rhetorical in what we call romance, and psychological in what we call realistic narrative" (Scholes and Kellogg, p. 188).[42]

Epic and romance clearly flourish today, although they, especially epic, are normally referred to simply as novels. Both can be distinguished from individuations by the worlds they present, the characters they portray, the nature and resolution of their conflicts, and by the language in which they are narrated. But what distinguishes epic and romance from each other? Scholes and Kellogg see the epic narrator as one who tells a traditional story; the epic is identified by its *mythos* or traditional plot (pp. 11-15). The idea of a traditional plot is a rather difficult one upon which to base a theory of genres, however. When stories are reduced to their basic elements, there are but a handful of plots in the entire history of narrative, and we can recognize an epic long before we know whether or not its story is traditional within the culture that produced it.

Epic and romance are similar in that both contain idealized, static worlds in which *kairos* is more important than *chronos*, both have inscrutable illustrative characters, and both offer conflicts between concepts or forces that are carefully controlled to insure the proper resolution. In the epic that conflict is of great national or social significance. Odysseus restores order and justice in Ithaka, Aeneas founds Rome, the Cid returns Spain to the Spanish and brings order back to the monarchy, Roland saves France, Vasco da Gama expands the Portuguese Empire and thus brings prosperity to his homeland. In romance the conflict takes on an aesthetic, ethical, or moral nature. Epic makes a commitment to the defense of political and social values; romance to the defense of spiritual values. Clearly, these values often overlap throughout history. The great defenders of the nation are seen as heroes of great moral stature. Patriotism is good and virtuous, while rebellion is evil. The epic, however, is far more likely to borrow from romance than vice versa. Romances tend to retain their purity, probably because their values are considered to be nobler and higher than mere political or social institutions.

---

[42]Bakhtin makes a number of extremely valuable distinctions of language in *The Dialogic Imagination.*

It is not uncommon for these three narrative forms, epic, romance, and individuation, to collide with each other in mid-composition, particularly in modern times. As the conflict develops, the author may be tempted either to take sides or to reverse an earlier position. This is particularly observable in younger nations in which authors are strongly influenced by the great European novelists, yet have political or moral axes to grind. The literary histories of such nations are particularly useful for observing the trajectory of these major narrative forms which are inextricably tied to cultural and political climates. The European literary tradition is so long and so familiar that we tend to think of the novel itself, including individuations, as a universal phenomenon that came along as a part of a natural historical process. While it is a part of a historical process, the fact that individuations are possible in England at the end of the eighteenth century does not mean they are possible at that time in the United States or in Latin America, or in Africa, or that they are even yet possible in many regions of the world, or that they can endure even in those nations where they have dominated the literary scene. As Todorov observes: "It is not chance that the epic is possible during one era, the novel during another (the individual hero of the latter being opposed to the collective hero of the former): each of these choices depends upon the ideological framework in which it operates."[43]

It is probably inevitable that authors of emerging nations where the problems and conflicts of a culture still maintain epic, heroic dimensions, will, because they have learned their craft not only from the great epic authors but also from the great novelists of Europe, mix their genres even though such synthesis is virtually impossible. While epic and romance may mix, because both uphold external value systems, neither combines well with the polar opposite, individuation. Spanish America provides a number of examples of such attempted syntheses in which the collision is readily observable because of the strength of the opposing elements. Many of these works have become classics that are read throughout the world, but European readers find them unsatisfactory and provincial precisely because of this unresolved tension.

---

[43]Tzvetan Todorov, "The Origen of Genres," *New Literary History*, 8.1 (Autumn 1976), 159-170.

A shining example of the violent clash between individuation and epic is the Venezuelan classic, *Doña Bárbara*. In this work Rómulo Gallegos set out to personify and animate the great clash that has dominated virtually all versions of Latin American cultural history: the forces of civilization and order versus the forces of barbarism and disorder. Clearly Gallegos, who later became president of Venezuela, will defend order. He made his hero a young lawyer, educated him in the capitol city, and named him Santos Luzardo (a combination of saint, light, and courage). In the opposing corner he placed an evil woman of dubious background and gave her the title role of Doña Bárbara, "bárbara" being the feminine adjective, barbarian. Santos Luzardo resides on the ranch Altamira (upward-looking) and Doña Bárbara on El miedo (fear).

In an epic with this scenario, Doña Bárbara would prove to be a worthy adversary, the two major characters would engage in a life-or-death struggle, and civilization would emerge, perhaps bloodied and weary, but victorious, and such is the case in this work. Nonetheless Gallegos commits a series of errors that threaten the unity of his narrative and leave it seriously flawed. Primary among these is that he endows the antagonist with a high degree of personality and gives her a convincing motivation for her barbarity. In fact, she is more convincing than her counterpart. The reader begins to understand her position and sympathize with it to the point that her personality takes control of the narrative. Gallegos, unlike the Argentinian Sarmiento, who while writing on the same theme in *Facundo* encountered the same problem but allowed his character to take control, insists on whipping the characters back into line. After a major fight in which Luzardo, the force of law and order, supposedly commits murder, Doña Bárbara, who still maintains her dominant position, simply abdicates. She herself sees that justice is done and then rides off into the swamp. Only one obstacle remains to the triumph of order over disorder, we now have a murderer for a hero. That problem is quickly resolved when one of Luzardo's men volunteers the information that he actually did the killing and that Luzardo's bullet missed.

It is difficult on the basis of these unlikely events to accept the idea that justice has been served and the cause of civilization advanced. What began as an epic soon became an individuation and would, perhaps, have been an excellent one could the author have restrained himself from interfering. But he wrote the work with a purpose, to advance and defend a political cause, and so intervened in an intolerable fashion to force his plot into line. Literary history is filled with such examples of epic, romance, and individuation in irresolvable conflict. The cause is clearly that authors want to write individuations, to create great, memorable *personalities*, yet they cannot or will not give up external control over the conflict. The desire to control means that a character within the work cannot become as important as the ideology the work espouses, or, if it does come to dominate, it must be because it represents, in an idealized version, that value. Such external manipulation is clearly antithetical to individuations. If the author does not choose between these extreme alternatives, the result will be badly flawed.

Another uneasy bedfellow of individuations that history has yielded is the picaresque tale. Frye argues that romance is dialectical because "everything is focussed on a conflict between the hero and his enemy, and all the reader's values are bound up with the hero" (*Anatomy of Criticism*, p. 187), but the same could be said of the epic, and if we modify the sentence to state that "many" or "most" rather than "all" of the reader's values are bound up with the hero, we have a description that fits individuations as well. All narrative is dialectical. In fact the concept of "conflict" dominates the discussion of narrative in all cultures but the Anglo-Saxon where it seems to be considered of lesser consequence. The picaresque tale is also dialectical but with an important difference from the three forms already discussed: while the reader may be amused by the antics of the pícaro and be entertained by his adventures, the reader's values are quite separate. In fact the pícaro seldom embodies any values whatsoever. He is not individualized and set in motion as is the hero of an individuation, he shows no human compassion or sentiment except in a most superficial way, and he does not develop or change as a result of his contacts and conflicts with the surrounding world. Claudio Guillén argues exactly the contrary, that "the picaresque *novel* . . . offers a process of conflict between the individual and his environment, inwardness and experience, whereby one element is not to be perceived without the other."[44] I do not believe Guillén's argument is valid. As Alastair Fowler observes, historically the picaresque is a

---

[44]Claudio Guillén, *Literature as System: Essays Toward the Theory of Literary History* (Princeton: Princeton University Press, 1971), p. 78.

totally different genre from novel, not a subclass.[45] In picaresque, the hero's role is largely syntactic; Todorov would term him the "copulative" that links episodes together (*Poetics of Prose*, p. 262). In individuations, transformations, not copulatives, span the episodes; there is a sense of cause and effect, of change and growth. The pícaro is no more human than are the heroes of epic and romance. Unlike the heroes of those two forms, rather than embodying values and advancing them, the pícaro exists to ridicule and deride the values of society. The picaresque tale is thus, as Scholes and Kellogg point out, inverted romance (*Nature of Narrative*, p. 75).

The picaresque tale is, in essence, a form of satire. What it shares with individuations is a dissatisfaction with social institutions, values, and customs. It is different in its manner of giving expression to those dissatisfactions. As Fowler argues, one genre can display certain features of another, yielding a subgenre. Thus an individuation could, because of certain traits of the protagonist or a loose, somewhat episodic structure, be described as "picaresque" so long as the major features of individuations were not violated. Subgenres retain the common features of the genre and add special additional features (*Kinds of Literature*, p. 112). Satire, like epic and romance, utilizes illustrative types in illustrative situations to achieve predetermined ends:

> There are novels, like *Rasselas* or *Animal Farm*, which rely on the diagrammatic rendering of types rather than the complex rendering of particulars, and these are the novels which we describe as tracts or satires rather than novels. They stand at the opposite pole from Lawrence, and their consistency is won at the expense of human vitality. This is not to denigrate their form, merely to distinguish it from the form of the true novel.[46]

---

[45] Alastair Fowler, *Kinds of Literature: An Introduction to the Theory of Genres and Modes* (Cambridge: Harvard University Press, 1982), p. 59.

[46] Barbara Hardy, *The Appropriate Form: An Essay on the Novel* (London: The Athlone Press, 1964), p. 172.

In recent years the cultivation of individuations has declined somewhat in English speaking countries and in France, although it certainly has not disappeared. Individuations have yielded, for a variety of reasons, to what Scholes calls "fabulation," particularly in the United States. Scholes discerns five distinct types of fabulation: romance, satire, picaresque, allegory, and epic--basic narrative forms from which individuations can and must be distinguished. Scholes uses the ancient fable as the basis for his term "fabulation" because he sees that most contemporary fiction has more in common with the fable than with realistic narrative: " . . . modern fabulation, like the ancient fabling of Aesop, tends away from the representation of reality but returns toward actual human life by way of ethically controlled fantasy. Many fabulators are allegorists. But the modern fabulators allegorize in particularly modern ways."[47]

The conflicts of fabulations are markedly different from those that characterize individuations: "Just as the realistic novel was rooted in the conflict between the individual and society, fabulation springs from the collision between the philosophical and mythic perspectives on the meaning and value of existence, with their opposed dogmas of struggle and acquiescence" (*Fabulators*, p. 173). Fabulation, like the narrative forms it embraces, is characterized by external control and design: "Delight in design, and its concurrent emphasis on the art of the designer, will serve in part to distinguish the art of the fabulator from the work of the novelist or satirist" (p. 10). External control of values, as we have seen, is antithetical to individuations, and external control of pattern is most difficult, for individuations seek to imitate life and life does not trace pleasing, symmetrical patterns. The reader with an eye for satisfying aesthetic form has reason to rejoice when he encounters such works as Joyce's *A Portrait of the Artist as a Young Man*, Rulfo's *Pedro Páramo*, Faulkner's *Absalom Absalom!*, or any other of the relatively scarce individuations in which content and form are fully synthesized into aesthetic patterns. External control of ideas and values yields forms that are not individuations--epics, romances, satires--but external control over design may still yield individuations even when the action seems somewhat forced. The difference lies in the fact that the author of an epic or a romance wishes to prove a point, to advance a conviction, and uses his characters and

----

[47]Robert Scholes, *The Fabulators* (New York: Oxford University Press, 1967), pp. 10-11.

their actions as illustrations, while in an individuation the author may attempt to control the action only because he wishes to create a pleasing structure.

There are undoubtedly a number of famous novelists who never produced an individuation. Many cultivate other genres, often extensively. Cervantes, for example, wrote only one individuation, *Don Quixote*, while some of the best-known contemporary novelists are better known for their non-individuations. John Fowles writes individuations (*Daniel Martin*) and other forms (*The Magus*), Gabriel García Márquez, both individuations (*No-one Writes to the Coronel*) and other genres (*One Hundred Years of Solitude*). It would be absurd to argue that one form is somehow superior to the others, but it is critical to recognize the difference.

New literary types emerge at least in large part because of changes in civilizations and cultures. Once such forms appear they may remain constantly present or may disappear even if only to reappear at a later time:

> ... there are clear social and historical relations between particular literary forms and the societies and periods in which they were originated or practised; [and] there are undoubted continuities of literary forms through and beyond the societies and periods to which they have such relations. In genre theory, everything depends on the character and process of such continuities.[48]

Harry Levin's perhaps overly-simplified statement on major narrative genres has a certain validity: "Epic, romance, and novel are the representatives of three successive estates and styles of life: military, courtly, and mercantile."[49] It is difficult at present to specify precisely the estate and style of life that has produced fabulation. Whatever the causes, they are surely related to the rapid growth of technology, the threats of impending world-wide disaster, and the loss of

----

[48]Raymond Williams, *Marxism and Literature* (Oxford: Oxford University Press, 1977), pp. 182-183.

[49]Levin, *The Gates of Horn: A Study of Five French Realists* (New York: Oxford University Press, 1963), p. 32.

man's identity and individuality. This loss is but one of the threats that face the survival of individuations.

Whatever the future, individuations emerged as a result, in part, of certain sociological conditions--conditions that appear in different cultures at different times, conditions that may change to such an extent as to make the form impossible, and conditions that have not yet even been met in many parts of the world. The novel has long been tied to the rise of the bourgeoisie in Europe, and for good reason: for the first time in history the conditions that make its primary form, individuations, viable, were widely and fully met. There are dangers inherent in assuming that the rise of the bourgeoisie was the only, or even the most important factor, however. The causes are so complex that they can perhaps never be fully and adequately explained in any single study:

> The theory of the novel as a bourgeois creation assumes that literature is a response to a sociological fact, institution or pattern; a response that can admittedly only be made by exceptionally talented individuals; but given the existence of such people, everything in the form and content can be adequately explained by contemporary social conditions. The idea of the romance as a source and origen of the novel produces a less simple picture, in which literature becomes more and society less important. It implies that both writers and readers are influenced not only by the social conditions but also by the books they read.[50]

Clearly writers are influenced by non-social factors and many could certainly be listed. When put together, however, they all are subsumed under cultural history. Within the flow of that history there are certain times in certain places in which certain basic requirements are met for the existence of certain literary forms. The basic requirements for individuations and their trajectory are the subject of this study. The territory has been made as broad as possible both in a temporal and a spatial sense because only by examining a variety of works and cultural situations can we test the validity of

----

[50]Diana Spearman, *The Novel and Society* (London: Routledge and Kegan Paul, 1966), p. 12.

this sociological theory. Concentration on one or two instances may be misleading simply because deeper causes may not become evident:

> Those who believe the modern novel first appeared in England and was a product of English life will feel the wind of liberty, discern the Puritan conscience and stress the importance of economic individualism. Those, on the other hand, who concentrate on French literature, will be apt to insist on the necessity of some kind of *elite*, the influence of a court, and the support which a small but educated audience gives to a writer. (Spearman, p. 55)

On the other hand, the discussion obviously must be limited. As Barthes points out, narrative analysis is:

> ... condemned to a deductive procedure obliged first to devise a hypothetical model of description (what American linguists call a 'theory') and then gradually work down from this model towards the different narrative species which at once conform to and depart from the model. It is only at the level of these conformities and departures that analysis will be able to come back to, but now equipped with a single descriptive tool, the plurality of narratives, to their historical, geographical and cultural diversity. (*Image-Music-Text*, p. 81)

The scope of this study must necessarily, then, be broad but limited, and the arguments often theoretical even though backed by specific illustration.

Individuation, to repeat earlier arguments, is a narrative form that offers highly individualized, believable, personalized human characters and their relationships to a specified, mimetic world. At its heart lies a belief in the value of the individual. Because of this belief, the character comes into conflict with the surrounding world which would mold and manipulate him or her. The plot of individuations is the trajectory of this struggle for supremacy, and the outcome is not so important as the struggle itself. Here my method clearly differs from those of Austin Wright and others who advance generic distinctions based on outcome. The nature of the struggle is more important than the outcome in recognizing individuations, and while pre-determined endings may be important in epic or romance, the variety of choices and the nature of the conflict in individuations restrict the usefulness of classifications based on endings.[51]

Because of the values individuations embody, it is evident that the form could not exist before society came to recognize the importance of individuality, and it cannot exist at any time, including today, if the value of the individual is denied. Furthermore, since the entire mechanism of the form is based on the collision between individual values and the values of others, and since reader and author sympathy gravitates most easily to the side that is most fully explored and best understood, i.e. that of the individual, individuations are not likely to be found in any society that is intolerant of dissent. This intolerance may take many forms-- a strong, coercive political system; social mores that are so firmly imbedded that the potential readers themselves will not accept any questioning of their convictions; a total unification of the society behind a common cause that cannot, at that point, be separated from the social institutions themselves; an unwillingness on the part of authors to criticize social institutions during times of grave crises; or any number of other causes that may contribute to the suppression of dissent.

During the course of this study the following topics will be given separate attention. Chapter Two examines in detail the nature of the individual/society relationship as it is manifested in individuations. Realism, verisimilitude, character individuality, and reader/character identification are stressed. Chapter Three surveys the historical significance of individuality in social, political, cultural, and literary contexts. Chapter Four attempts to synthesize the contents of Two and Three to reveal the role of the author of individuations as a dissident voice, a particularly dangerous critic of the *status quo*. Chapter Five delineates the incompatability of the form with certain social and political conditions: feudalism, neoclassicism, totalitarianism, and colonialism. For contrast, it compares these conditions with those that have allowed individuations to flourish in certain cultures. The conclusion examines contemporary conditions and speculates on the present and future of individuation as a form.

---

[51] Austin M. Wright, *The Formal Principle in the Novel* (Ithaca: Cornell University Press, 1982).

CHAPTER TWO

Character/Society/Conflict

Individuation, as we have seen, has as its core the individual human being, and as Henry James argues, "we know a man imperfectly until we know his society, and we but half know a society until we know its manners."[1] We might add that we cannot know a person, nor can we understand society in the abstract; both must be made sufficiently specific for us to recognize them and believe in them. They must be mimetic. The argument seems legitimately circular: to know the individual, we must first know his or her society; to understand society we must know the particulars concerning its manners; these particulars can be revealed only through social action in process; society in process is the interaction of individuals. It is impossible to separate clearly these elements--man, society, interaction--yet they can be more fully understood if examined in isolation. The lowest common denominator is clearly the individual.

Character has probably received more attention and generated more comment than any other ingredient of the novel, simply because action and setting have no meaning without it. We could conceivably have a character sketch without much reference to action or setting, but action without characters is inconceivable. We might also have descriptions of physical settings without character, but as soon as society becomes an aspect of setting, so too do characters. The novel form gave literary artists the opportunity to explore character more fully than any previous type of literature: "As a vehicle for individualism, it was free to concentrate on character, with wider variety and richer detail than previous fiction."[2] Character came to be the great love of the reading public, and Virginia Woolf speaks for the majority when she sees it as the cornerstone of the novel:

---

[1] Henry James, "Emerson," in *The Art of Fiction and Other Essays* (New York: Oxford University Press, 1948), p. 221.

[2] Harry Levin, *The Gates of Horn: A Study of Five French Realists* (New York: Oxford University Press, 1963), p. 36.

> I believe that all novels . . . deal with character, and that it is to express character--not to preach doctrines, sing songs, or celebrate the glories of the British Empire, that the form of the novel, so clumsy, verbose, and undramatic, so rich, elastic, and alive, has been evolved.[3]

This passion for character, coupled with the popularity of the novel form and serial publication, led not only to mass grieving for the deaths of characters in the nineteenth century, but to reader influence on the action, phenomena that have only recently been equalled in television soap operas.

Scholars have gone to a great deal of effort to analyse and classify character types. Forster distinguishes only two--flat and round. Others have used "developed" and "undeveloped," "interiorized" and "non-interiorized", and the like, and from a slightly different perspective, "foreground" and "background", etc.. W.J. Harvey has made useful distinctions among various types that fall into three major categories: protagonists, background, and intermediate. The protagonists are naturally the most important, but they are also the most difficult to discuss as literary creations. It is easier and generally more profitable to discuss them as human beings: "they are what the novel exists for; it exists to reveal them . . . . it is unwise to generalize about them; each exists as an individual case and demands special consideration."[4] The two additional classes of character: background and intermediate, are important because they give specificity and immediacy to the other great force in indivuduations, society. Individuations seem unable to exist without them, for they represent one of the two forces that must collide to give birth to the form. Defoe, however, proved that such is not the case. *Robinson Crusoe* would be an individuation without the introduction of Friday. The cannibals create excitement and suspense, and Friday adds interest, but the forces of a civilized environment are present on the island long before Crusoe discovers footprints in the sand, for the protagonist brings them with him. His preoccupation with physical comforts, the pas-

----

[3] Virginia Woolf, "Mr. Bennett and Mrs. Brown," in *Approaches to the Novel: Materials for a Poetics*, ed. Robert Scholes, rev. ed. (San Francisco: Chandler Publishing Co., 1966), p. 193.
[4] W.J. Harvey, *Character and the Novel* (Ithaca, New York: Cornell University Press, 1965), p. 56.

sage of time, and above all, with finances and writing, represent society far more effectively than the addition of uncivilized characters.

Other novelists have demonstrated that one can write an individuation without a solitary protagonist. It is probably the lack of a clear-cut forefront character around whom all major actions revolve that causes Henry James and Percy Lubbock to have misgivings about *War and Peace*, which offers the reader several fully-developed characters, each of whom is as carefully individualized as the main character of most novels that contain but one protagonist.

Behind the protagonists, background characters provide society its vitality, its depth and its breadth:

> ... social setting is one of the most important of all human contexts, and while the novelist can do a great deal by way of direct description and analysis, society must also be seen as a complex web of *individual* relationships. This is most economically achieved by establishing a range of background characters whose individuality need be no more than is adequate to typify social trends or pressures . . . . (Harvey, p. 56)

Background characters can thus be symbolic and be manipulated; a protagonist cannot: "the more he *stands for* the less he *is* . . ." (Harvey, p. 67).

Even so, there is a need for protagonists not to become so individual, so eccentric, as to be unrecognizable as worldly human beings. Plausibility is crucial despite, perhaps because of, the great potential for variety in portraying human characters. Even highly developed protagonists may be "types," as Lukács insists,[5] but, as Erich Auerbach points out, the reader does not view them as such: "what we see is the concrete individual figure with its own physique and its own history . . . ."[6] What we recognize in individuations is the type

---

[5] Georgy Lukács, *Studies in European Realism: A Sociological Survey of the Writings of Balzac, Stendhal, Zola, Tolstoy, Gorki, and Others*, trans. Edith Bone (London: Hillway Publishing Co., 1950), see especially pp. 54-55.

[6] Erich Auerbach, *Mimesis: The Representation of Reality in Western Literature*, trans. Willard R. Trask (Princeton: Princeton University Press, 1968), p. 475.

through the individual. We can never reverse the process. If *Tom Jones* must be excluded it is for precisely this reason; none of the characters becomes adequately individualized. Fielding prefers categorized characters, as their names reflect. Tom Jones represents every man, "in accordance with his creator's purpose to show 'not men, but manners; not an individual, but a species.'"[7] It is the individuality of characters that engages our emotions in great novels, and we become emotionally involved with them because we believe in them as human beings, "we feel a strong concern for the characters as people; we care about their good and bad fortune."[8] The capability of the novel form to generate our concern for specific, individual human beings and for their interactions with other human beings makes the process of individuation possible, to the point that "we may legitimately talk of the reality of fictional characters" (Harvey, p. 52).

Individuality of character brings with it, out of necessity, a degree of independence which is carefully controlled, not by the author, but by the various social and physical circumstances that the author affords to the characters. Plausibility is an absolute necessity: "Unless his characters act and think at all points consistently with the laws of their imagined existence, and unless these laws are in harmony with the laws of actual life, no amount of sophistication on the part of the author can make us finally believe his story...."[9] Characters endowed with a high degree of individuality, thus bound only by believability and circumstance, may, indeed must if they are to maintain their integrity, pass beyond the absolute control and manipulations of the author. Eduardo Mallea, in admonishing budding novelists, warned that "You should give obeisance to nothing more than the profound truth of your creatures: if they are strong, they will rebel against you yourself in every way; all you have to do is listen to them faithfully."[10] Ninety years earlier, Anthony Trollope

---

[7]Ian Watt, *The Rise of the Novel: Studies in Defoe, Richardson and Fielding* (Berkeley and Los Angeles: University of California Press, 1967), p. 272.

[8]Wayne C. Booth, *The Rhetoric of Fiction* (Chicago: University of Chicago Press, 1961), pp. 129-130.

[9]Clayton Meeker Hamilton, *The Art of Fiction: A Formulation of Its Fundamental Principles* (New York: Doubleday, Doran & Company, Inc., 1939), p. 12.

[10]"A nada deberá servir más que a la verdad profunda de sus criaturas: si son fuertes, de todos modos se rebelarán sobre usted mismo; sólo le tocará escuc-

too had argued that the novelist must know his characters intimately: "He must learn to hate them and to love them. He must argue with them, quarrel with them, forgive them, and even submit to them."[11]

This individuality, this degree of independence, is the principle reason that structuralism has had to avoid the issue of highly-developed characters:

> ... the general ethos of structuralism runs counter to the notions of individuality and rich psychological coherence which are often applied to the novel. Stress on the interpersonal and conventional systems which traverse the individual, which make him a space in which forces and events meet rather than an individuated essence, leads to a rejection of a prevalent conception of character in the novel: that the most successful and 'living' characters are richly delineated autonomous wholes, clearly distinguished from others by physical and psychological characteristics. This notion of character, structuralists would say, is a myth.[12]

Myth or no, readers have for centuries, and continue today to view the characters of novels in this light of "richly delineated autonomous wholes," but once again subject to the same restrictions as any one of us:

> The greatness of the genre ... has been to present to us ... lives that might seem like our lives, minds like our minds, desires like our own desires. That has been what most novelists quite clearly have tried to accomplish in their writing, and that is what still makes the reading of novels for most people, intellectuals included, one of the perennially absorbing activities of modern culture.[13]

---

harlas con lealtad." Eduardo Mallea, *Poderío de la novela* (Buenos Aires: Aguilar, 1965), p. 92.

[11]Anthony Trollope, *An Autobiography* (Berkeley and Los Angeles: University of California Press, 1947), p. 194.

[12]Jonathan Culler, *A Structuralist Poetics: Structuralism, Linguistics and the Study of Literature* (Ithaca: Cornell University Press, 1975), p. 230.

[13]Robert Alter, *Motives for Fiction* (Cambridge and London: Harvard Univer-

The restrictions placed on human beings, on characters, on "us" are often thought of in terms of natural law. All are subject to heat and cold, physical limitations of strength, disease, the process of aging, etc., but the barriers most typical of individuations are not these, although they may be not only present but important, but those restrictions that emerge as a result of social situation and interaction between the character and fellow characters.

Thus Stephen Daedalus' poor eyesight and physical weakness are important, but these need not be overcome: they serve to isolate him from the other boys. *A Portrait of the Artist as a Young Man* is not the story of a sickly youth who overcomes physical disabilities, but that of a sensitive, isolated young man who confronts the larger issues of aesthetics, patriotism, morality, and his own identity. Young Pip in *Great Expectations* is limited at first by his social and economic status, later by his ambition and false pride, and it is the process of his maturation and his discovery of truer values that make the novel so powerful. This work by itself stands as a definitive rebuttal to all who classify Dickens as a mere caricaturist, and disproves Northrop Frye's charge that Dickens writes only "fairy tales in the low mimetic mode."[14]

The conquering of great physical barriers, be they mountains, jungles, oceans, or even physical handicaps, is more in tune with the characteristics of the epic than with individuation. The struggles of the latter tend toward the less grandiose and the more personal. For this reason, the heroes of individuations are seldom heroic--they are solitary individuals struggling through the problems of everyday life. No novel ever offered more opportunity for true heroics than does *War and Peace*, yet no study of grave crises in politics and on the battlefield ever demonstrated more clearly that even the most significant actions of the most legendary of men are but the result of thousands of fortuitous, petty circumstances that just happen to coalesce at the proper moment. Individuations such as *War and Peace* are not interested in the great exploits of man but in the small, personal, in perspective even petty, struggles of everyday life.

---

sity Press, 1984), p. 21.

[14]Northrop Frye, "Dickens and the Comedy of Humors," in *Experience in the Novel: Selected Papers from the English Institute*, ed. Roy Harvey Pearce (New York: Columbia University Press, 1968), p. 49.

Unlike epics, such works never draw our attention away from the character to the event; the event is significant because it affords us the opportunity to observe its effect on the character. We care for nothing so much as we care for the individuals and their progress. The nature of individual characters and the manner in which they are presented and developed are critical issues in individuations, but they progress by means of and their progress is measured by their interactions with society: "By far the most important of contexts is the web of human relationships in which any single character must be enmeshed" (Harvey, p. 52). Because their characters are individualized, with essences and actions that are believable and mimetic, individuations tend to be highly ambiguous. As circumstances change so do the characters, and the changes in the characters lead to further alterations of the circumstances, especially the social contexts.

The individual is not of interest, indeed cannot even exist, in total isolation. Even *Robinson Crusoe* is composed of three major conflicting forces: the isolated protagonist, the forces of untamed nature with which he must contend, and the values and forces of civilization which he brings with him. The plot of the novel is the history of reconciliation among these three forces, the attempts by Crusoe to bring them into harmony. Measuring, identifying, and opposing the individual are all remaining elements. Just as the characters are individualized, so too are their circumstances: "the novel is surely distinguished . . . by the amount of attention it habitually accords both to the individualisation of its characters and to the detailed presentation of their environment" (Watt, pp. 17-18). In fact, the individualization of characters and the particularization of environment go hand in hand; each is dependent upon the other: "the characters of the novel can only be individualised if they are set in a background of particularised time and place" (Watt, p. 21).

Obviously among the most important of possible circumstances are the other characters, some standing as other individuals at crossroads with the main character or characters. Many novels have no true main character, but a number of individuals, each in search of a personal future, that bump into one another, now in conflict, now in momentary harmony. Lesser characters may represent particularized forces of society and be present only to give voice to a specific value or attitude. The creation of multitudes of such characters was one of Dicken's greatest achievements, yet became the major cause of attacks on his work. The group of characters in a novel, a group that is sometimes small, sometimes massive, depicts above all the social circumstances of the more representational figures; the characters are present as themselves, but also as small portions of society.

The individuated character with personal needs is important, the society in which those needs must be fulfilled is important, but so too are physical setting and the world of physical objects. In descriptions, the novel appears similar to the epic, but it can be distinguished from its historical predecessor. The lengthy descriptions of the novel, particularly those of the nineteenth century, have been well defended. A character was identified and held in high or low esteem frequently on the basis of physical possesions, which reflected wealth or poverty, good taste or poor, and moral and aesthetic values. As in the epic, in the novel specific details are in great demand:

> The epic ... is the form of all literary forms closest to the novel; it has the 'boiler-plate,' the lists and catalogues, the circumstantiality, the concern with numbers and dimensions. The epic geography, like that of the novel, can be *mapped*, in both the physical and the social sense.[15]

But there is a significant difference between the objects of the epic world and those of individuations: in the latter, objects, like the characters themselves, have become problematic. In the epic world man is in harmony with his possessions. The hero is untouched by the petty squabblings of inferiors over prizes and rewards. The epic hero is likely to have a sturdy ship, a magnificent horse, vastly superior weapons, and so on down to the smallest detail. The hero of an individuation tends to be at odds with possessions--they are inadequate, inferior, or if such is not the case he or she is not satisfied with them or may even be their prisoner. Rarely can one find in Homeric literature an instance in which the hero is dissatisfied with possesions--the hero of individuations more often than not is. Objects in Homer reflect the hero's ideal world. In individuations they reflect either the plainness or poverty of that world, or if they are objects of value, they stand to demonstrate the hero's dissatisfaction even with them. Homeric man stood in close relation to his objects--he made them himself,

---

[15]Mary McCarthy, "The Fact in Fiction," *Partisan Review*, 27.3 (Summer 1960), p. 450.

or raised them, or oversaw their production. Modern man (the hero of individuations) has no such close relationship. He purchases them and a series of unknown persons is responsible for their production.[16] Setting is thus critically related to character. As Hamilton points out, character comments on background and background on character. They are inextricable (*The Art of Fiction*, pp. 140-160).

Just as setting and its relationship to the main characters can be used to distinguish individuation from epic, so too can it be helpful in distinguishing the genre from romance, where, as in epic, objects are in harmony with their possessors. As Swingewood points out, Utopian fiction deals with perfection, with harmony. "... unlike the nineteenth-century realist novel, utopias have no problematic hero, their structures are not dominated by a deep sense of conflict between the individual and society."[17] There is no conflict, no pressure for change, because there is no need for change in an already perfect world. In individuations, conflict and change, be that change in the character or in the circumstances, are all-important: "The individual stands in opposition to society, but he is nourished by it. And it is far less important to know what differentiates him than what nourishes him. Like the genius, the individual is valuable for what there is within him."[18] The story of this interaction gives individuation both its plot and its force.

It would be extremely difficult, if not impossible, to reduce conflict to a definitive body of types. Attempts to systematize literature always seem least effective when they deal with the novel because it seeks to imitate life in its full complexity. Once the personality of the character and the nature of that character's circumstances are established, the conflict may go in any direction. This is not to say that the novelist may not have an *a priori* major conflict to explore, but that once the wheels are set in motion a kinetic force takes hold which may move the action in unforeseen directions. Alvin J. Seltzer

---

[16] For an excellent discussion of Hegel's and Lukács' studies of objects in Homer and modern literature see David H. Miles, "Portrait of the Marxist as a Young Hegelian: Lukács' *Theory of the Novel*," *PMLA*, 94.3 (Jan. 1979), 22-35.

[17] Alan Swingewood, *The Novel and Revolution* (Great Britain: Barnes & Noble, 1975), p. 143.

[18] Andre Malraux, Preface to *Days of Wrath*, trans. Haakon M. Chevalier (New York: Random House, 1936), p. 6.

has defined five basic ways, or levels at which novels may examine life, each of which is definable in terms of conflict: 1) Inner conflict--man's struggle to find his identity, the battle with his own soul; 2) Conscious conflict-- man's attempt to create meaning and beauty and a value system; 3) Social conflict--man's struggle with society and with political systems, a clash of visions of man; 4) Human conflict--one man against another, love, hate, etc.; 5) Spiritual conflict--man's confrontation with the universe.[19] Additional categories could surely be suggested and these five could be further refined, amplified, and sub-categorized, perhaps yielding a deeper understanding of the complex possibilities of the novel form, but it seems more profitable and even more accurate to discard the whole system. What, precisely, is the difference between inner conflict and spiritual conflict? As man struggles to find his identity does he not struggle to find his relative place in the universe and for that matter in society? And does the concept of identity and relative significance not also suggest the recognition and acceptance of a value system? And finally, how are these to be isolated from human conflict--my values, my conception of my identity against all who would attack, deride, or otherwise infringe upon them? Claude Bremond's attempt to classify narratives according to a Proppian system of functions in order to create a "map of the logical possibilities of narrative" is imposing, but offers little of use for a better understanding of the possibilities of individuations.[20]

What matters most in individuations are: 1) the human individuals; 2) all forces including other characters external to those individuals; and 3) the dialectical interrelationship between 1 and 2. As we have seen, no one in real life and no one in an individuation can ever be entirely isolated. Even Crusoe carries society within him. Man must be seen through his relations with others, as Virginia Woolf points out: "if as novelist you wish to test man in all his relationships, the proper antagonist is man; his ordeal is in society, not solitude."[21] The struggling forces at the heart of every individuation are but two; the inner world of the individual versus everything else, even

---

[19] Alvin J. Seltzer, *Chaos in the Novel--The Novel in Chaos* (New York: Schocken Books, 1974), pp. 2-3.

[20] Claude Bremond, "The Logic of Narrative Possibilities," *New Literary History*, 11.3 (Spring 1980), 387-411.

[21] Virginia Woolf, "Joseph Conrad," in *The Common Reader* (New York: Harcourt, Brace and Company, 1925), p. 316.

though this essential conflict may often be interpreted in different lights and with different stresses. Georgy Lukács describes it as abstract versus concrete potentiality:

> Abstract potentiality belongs wholly to the realm of subjectivity; whereas concrete potentiality is concerned with the dialectic between the individual's subjectivity and objective reality. The literary presentation of the latter thus implies a description of actual persons inhabiting a palpable, identifiable world.[22]

Even though at the heart of individuations we thus find a duality of the individual against the world, this is not sufficient to define the genre. Watt points out that the works of Marlowe and Defoe demonstrate this duality: "all tends to resolve itself into an *ego contra mundum*" (*Rise of the Novel*, pp. 131-132), but this resolution is certainly a hallmark of the picaresque tale as well.

A further distinction between the picaresque and individuation is that the picaresque is seldom capable of pathos because the reader's emotions are rarely engaged by the antics of the pícaro or by his personality, which tends to be overly amorphous, even though both genres stress similar conflicts:

> The root idea of pathos is the exclusion of an individual on our own level from a social group to which he is trying to belong. Hence the central tradition of sophisticated pathos is the study of the isolated mind, the story of how someone recognizably like ourselves is broken by a conflict between the inner and outer world, between imaginative reality and the sort of reality which is established by a social consensus.[23]

---

[22] Georgy Lukács, "The Ideology of Modernism," in *The Meaning of Contemporary Realism*, trans. John and Necke Mander (London: Merlin Press, 1963), pp. 23-24.

[23] Northrop Frye, *Anatomy of Criticism: Four Essays* (New York: Atheneum, 1967), p. 39.

We can make an even more significant distinction, however, by observing the differences in the courses the conflicts follow: "The special genius of the novel as a genre is its ability to depict not only the exterior world of action, but the interior world of character--and one crucial thing more, the relation between them."[24] The interaction between self and world and the resulting constant change comprises a major characteristic that separates individuation and the traditional novel from picaresque tale, and to a large degree determines content. What happens is not so much action as interaction (See Friedman, pp. 10-11).

Another distinction can now be made between picaresque tale and individuation. Interaction requires a particular conception of temporal flow, of *chronos*. Because the picaresque is not sensitive to interaction, to a sense of constant growth and change, it is episodic. Individuation may be episodic only to a degree. Even in those works in which time is deliberately disjointed and shuffled we can, indeed we are forced in the process of reading, to recognize the developing pattern of cause and effect, conflict and change. *Don Quixote* is highly episodic, yet across the episodes the personalities evolve, the episodes themselves become less ridiculous and more explicable in terms of our own concept of reality, and even the tone of the narrator softens as the characters gain our sympathy and understanding. The trajectory of the interaction, seen through time, made possible by time, is critical: "It is the narrative interaction--that is, in time, in the storyteller's own good time--between the subjective and the objective worlds that creates what we call the novel" (Friedman, p. xiv).

All these elements: the characters, their circumstances, the ebb and flow of their daily living, are thus mimetic and natural. There is in individuations a delicate sense of balance between individual and society, a balance that is especially evident in the major and most typical novels of what is called the "realist tradition," as Raymond Williams has argued.[25] The reader will generally gravitate toward greater sympathy for the individual, perhaps not because he or she is more valuable, but because the reader comes to know and understand

----

[24]Alan Friedman, *The Turn of the Novel: The Transition to Modern Fiction* (London, Oxford, New York: Oxford University Press, 1966), p. xiv.

[25]Raymond Williams, *The Long Revolution* (New York: Columbia University Press, 1961), pp. 278-279.

the character so well. The possibility of this sympathetic understanding of the value of both the individual and society and their interrelations is a product of evolving cultural history and subject to modification: "The eighteenth-century novel is formally most like our own, under comparable pressures and uncertainties, and it was in the deepening understanding of the relations between individuals and societies that the form actually matured" (Williams, p. 279).

This delicate balance is in part sustained by the fact that each individual is not only a private person but a public one as well, the public person becoming either a mask to hide the true individual or an attempt to reconcile his or her claims with those of society. Conflicts between individuals are also conflicts between social values, again preserving a degree of balance between opposing loyalties. Within the novelistic tradition, the balance is often tipped slightly to one side or the other. Harvey argues that novels in which the scale is balanced are realistic. If greater weight is given to to world, the result is naturalism, and if the individual is stressed, the novel is subjective (*Character and the Novel*, pp. 133-134). These arguments require some refining to be useful here. In naturalistic individuations, the world is more important not in an idealistic sense but in a sense of power and domination. Readers still tend to identify with the main characters, who are helpless against the power of the world. Such works are typified by an external objective view of the world as a great machine overpowering the relatively helpless individual. Subjective individuations see the conflict not only from the perspective of but from within the individual.

When one of the two sides involved in the balance is given priority in terms of value, the generic consequences are more obvious. If the world, or society, is given greater value, the work tends to become epic, even though the characters may not be as heroic as those we associate with that genre. If the character has greater value and has a developed personality, individuation prevails. Or, if the character is not developed and the imbalance is extreme, satire or the picaresque results. In any case of extreme imbalance, the characters tend to be less than fully individualized, and both Self and World less realistically drawn. In *Tom Jones*, for example, the stress on societal values and the unrealistic, almost *deus ex machina* events that make it possible to establish the proper order and bring all to a happy conclusion move the work toward the epic tradition despite all the picaresque overtones of the protagonist and his actions. *Tom Jones* is largely neoclassical in spirit; order is restored in the universe, but to the sacrifice of verisimilitude and of a sense of the individual as autonomous and free. Fielding's characters do not change through interaction; they are defined and must then simply be consistent. His works are not individuations.

While a sense of balance between Self and World is most typical of the nineteenth-century European tradition, Raymond Williams has traced a separation within this realist tradition into the "social" and the "personal" novel (*Long Revolution*, pp. 279-280), and a further development of the latter into the "novel of personal formula" (p. 283). Individuation falls within this line of narrative development: We can say of novels in this class that they take only one person seriously, but then ordinarily very seriously indeed . . . . A world is actualized on one man's senses: not narrated, or held at arm's length, but taken as it is lived" (p. 283).

This type of fiction, although it is quite removed from the traditional realistic novel, is a natural development within the genre, and continues the tradition of individuation. The "psychological" novel belongs here as well. On the opposite side of the coin, there are a number of great novels that are not devoted to the full depiction and development of character. The objections to *Vanity Fair* shared by James and Lubbock are in part due to that work's lack of a major dominating central character, just as they had reservations concerning *War and Peace* on the same score. Lubbock argues that *Vanity Fair* is not the story of any one or two characters, but of the group--"the story they unite to tell"--and goes on to term it "not a portrait of character but a panorama of manners."[26] It is true that *Vanity Fair* lacks a strong central character, but it has a number of convincing, independent ones, as well as a fully protrayed society and a continuous sense of interaction and change, characteristics that place it squarely within the tradition of individuation.

At the heart of the distinction lies, once again, the concept of the human individual and its value, not as a symbol but as an essence:

----

[26]Percy Lubbock, *The Craft of Fiction* (New York: The Viking Press, 1957), p. 95 and p. 118.

> The world of the novel is not substantial.... it is dominated by *the duality of the Self and the external world*. This duality means that the individual is neither the direct personification of the prevalent forces in the described sphere of existence, nor are the self-objectifications of the hero immediately given, in forms that can be appropriated and used.[27]

The major characters in *Vanity Fair* are not present merely as personifications of social forces. Even Becky stirs compassion when she is violently confronted by Rawdon in Chapter 53, and when everyone subsequently deserts her, even though she deserves the scorn she now receives. Amelia is also complex for she lacks that stable state of purity that she would seem to represent at the outset. Both are characters typical of individuations.

Individuation, like the life it imitates, is highly ambiguous. Characters, at least major ones, cannot be pure virtue or pure evil, and while the author may certainly take sides to a degree in the major conflicts, any attempt to load the dice or use the conflict to preach a doctrine will damage the work or create something other than an individuation. Many individuations begin with clear issues, but as the conflict begins to grow and develop, authorial interference must not inhibit the action or the characters from running their courses:

> The characters created by the great realists, once conceived in the vision of their creator, live an independent life of their own: their comings and goings, their development, their destiny is dictated by the inner dialectic of their social and individual existence. No writer is a true realist--or even a truly good writer, if he can direct the evolution of his own characters at will. (Lukács, *Studies in European Realism*, p. 11)

Scholes and Kellogg identify two types of dynamic characterization: the developmental, which follows a plot line based on ethical considerations, and the chronological, which is more purely temporal.[28] E.M.

----

[27] Ferenc Fehér, "Is the Novel Problematic? A Contribution to the Theory of the Novel," *Telos*, 15 (1973), p. 51.

[28] Robert Scholes and Robert Kellogg, *The Nature of Narrative* (London, Oxford, New York: Oxford University Press, 1968), p. 169.

Forster's distinction of "life by time" and "life by values" is essentially the same (*Aspects of the Novel*, p. 28), as is Muir's life "in Time, personally, and in Space, socially."[29] Whatever the terminology, it is clear that the concept of mimesis, so central to that form of the novel we have called individuation, when coupled with conflict, will require a resulting sense of change in the character. As Friedman puts it, "Every central character must in a sense relative to his story, be *relatively* innocent at the beginning of his book: that is, he must be more innocent earlier in the story than he is later in the story" (*Turn of the Novel*, p. 7). The *Bildungsroman* is an obvious application of this basic concept.

The final change in a character, or a final comprehensive grasp of the full nature of his or her changed personality, is more often than not less interesting and less significant to the plot than the process of give and take involved in the individual's dealings with the world. As characters change and mature, they become increasingly well-defined and "real" for the reader who shares their experiences and increasing understanding. This is a major aspect of the process of individuation. Percy Lubbock observes this dynamic, realistic sense of change in Tolstoi, and despite his reservations concerning *War and Peace*, admires the developmental characters: "They grow as we all do, they change in the only possible direction, that which results from the clash between themselves and their conditions" (*Craft of Fiction*, p. 51). George Orwell sees this power as a major point of contrast between the Russian novelist and Dickens: "he is writing about people who are growing. His characters are struggling to make their souls, whereas Dickens's are already finished and perfect."[30] Here again *Great Expectations* provides evidence of Dickens' ability to create truly dynamic characters, although Pip's maturation is somewhat cloaked by the narrative point of view, which is that of a fully mature Pip looking back with some discomfort on his youth. This sense of change is one of the most important keys to individuations, again because it is mimetic. One debilitating consequence of determinism, when seen at its extreme, is that there is little or no struggle, and no change. The characters and their personal characteristics have no

---

[29] Edwin Muir, *The Structure of the Novel* (New York: Harcourt, Brace and Company, 1929), p. 63.

[30] George Orwell, "Charles Dickens," in *A Collection of Essays by George Orwell* (New York: Harcourt Brace Jovanovich, Inc., 1953), p. 99.

form-determining dialectical relationship with the outside world.

Not only the nature of the conflict and the contrasting forces then, but the progress of the clash and its effects are extremely important to individuations, which in this as in all else, must be mimetic. This need for verisimilitude and inner consistency significantly reduces the novelist's options as the work moves toward a conclusion. There may still be a wide variety of possible courses for the action to take, but if the author envisions a particular resolution from the outset, he or she may be in difficulty at the end, for if a writer has followed the characters and their actions rather than lead, major improbabilities may be required to get the story back in line. In romance and epic improbability and an occasional instance of *deus ex machina* are within the rules, indeed expected, but in individuations they may be disastrous.

On an obvious yet important level, the action may take one of two courses: conciliation between individual and society or rejection. In other words, the work may be what Frye would term tragic or comic, depending upon how it is concluded. Either ending is perfectly possible and appropriate, as is a totally ambiguous ending, which often is the most mimetic of all. Because of the high value individuations place on individualism, Frye's "tragic" conclusions are often among the most optimistic, while those he would term "comic" may be disheartening to the reader. *Don Quixote* must be termed comic, for the hero dies a sane man, securely back in the good graces of society, and defending societal values. The reader, however, is with those who plead for him to return to madness. Conversely, *A Portrait of the Artist* concludes happily for Stephen and the reader, for the protagonist succeeds in liberating himself from all societal strictures. Not until we read *Ulysses* do we find that this liberation was indeed unhappy for Stephen. In an epic there is no possibility of a tragic ending, or even for an unhappy comic one. The hero *is* society and its values. The hero who is outcast is simply misunderstood or the victim of inferiors. As the people of Burgos declare in *The Poem of the Cid*, "Were his lord but worthy, God how fine a vassal!"[31]

---

[31]"Dios, que buen vassallo, si oviesse buen senore!," *Poema de Mio Cid*, ed. Ramón Menéndez Pidal (Madrid: Espasa-Calpe, S.A., 1966), p. 105. The translation is by W.S. Merwin, in *Medieval Epics* (New York: Random House, Inc. 1963), p. 470.

Traditional narrative before the novel was bound by myth, ritual, and festival, in which, as in the epic, society is preserved. Rebellion by the individual is not tolerated:

> Social duties continue the lesson of the festival into normal, everyday existence, and the individual is validated still. Conversely, indifference, revolt--or exile--break the vitalizing connections. From the standpoint of the social unit, the broken-off individual is simply nothing--waste. Whereas the man or woman who can honestly say that he or she has lived the role--whether that of priest, harlot, queen, or slave---*is* something in the full sense of the verb *to be*.[32]

Individuations often violate this traditional principle. They suggest that the individual truly *is* something only when he or she rebels against the restrictions of society and defends personal values.

The important point insofar as maintaining the integrity of the novel form is not whether or no the individual is reconciled with society, but whether the ending is continuous and consistent with the history of the conflict, whether it has been properly prepared. Stephen Daedalus seeks escape, and achieves it. Julien Sorel seeks acceptance to another social class, and when it is nearly within his grasp, rejects it. Henderson (*Henderson the Rain King*) is simply looking for a satisfactory niche, but does not find it. Young Pip seeks a niche and finds it, but it is not the one that he sought, even though it is morally superior to what he desired.

Also important to the integrity of individuations is that the conclusion not be certain from an early point in the narrative. Since the form imitates life, the future cannot be absolutely certain. In the epic, we know from the beginning that the hero will triumph. The story provokes interest not because we wish to know how it will all turn out, but because we are interested to see what happens before the conclusion, and to relish in the details that verify our expectations. Again, *Tom Jones* is exemplary of the epic nature of many novels:

---

[32]Joseph Campbell, *The Hero with a Thousand Faces* (Cleveland: World Publishing Company, 1956), pp. 383-384.

> Though we do not know exactly *how* the story will be resolved, the personality of the narrator encourages an expectation that it *will* be resolved, happily for the sympathetic characters, and less happily for the unsympathetic. The whole novel thus serves as a metaphor for the providence of a just and benevolent God who, in the end, in His own way and in *His* own good time, may be trusted to make an equitable distribution of rewards and punishments.[33]

In some individuations, such as *The Death of Ivan Ilyich* or *The Death of Artemio Cruz*, we know from the beginning how the action will conclude. The body of the narrative, however, is the history of how such a conclusion came about and an exploration and justification of the character. In epic, the character needs no such delineation, for all that the hero is or does is already justified by he or she who does it. The resolution of the conflict in an individuation must then be in doubt for the majority of the story, and must be believable. It must seem the natural consequence of what has taken place before. It is most difficult for a writer to maintain total control over conflict once he or she has created strong individual characters and specific societal forces and set them in motion. It is nearly impossible to impose a conclusion that will accomplish any goal other than the satisfactory, believable conclusion of the story that has been followed.

The most common and grave aesthetic flaw found in novels is didacticism, a characteristic incompatible with individuation. A great many writers of talent have sought to use the novel form to preach their views. Only those who are superior artists have been able to allow ambiguity to creep in and the story to determine its own conclusion. As Tolstoy maintains:

> The goals of art are incommensurate (as mathematicians say) with social goals. The goal of the artist is not to solve a question irrefutably, but to force people to love life in all its innumerable, inexhaustible manifestations. If I were told that I could write a novel in which I should set forth the apparently correct attitudes toward all social questions, I

---

[33]David Lodge, "The Uses and Abuses of Omniscience," in *The Novelist at the Crossroads and Other Essays on Fiction and Criticism* (Ithaca: Cornell University Press, 1971), p. 123.

would not devote even two hours of work to such a novel....[34]

Novels of overt social protest, theses, etc., seldom survive as art, no matter how lofty their purpose or how great their impact in their own time. Frank Norris is nearly unreadable today, as are most works of social realism. This is due in part to the authors' greater concern with a thesis than with art, but also to the fact that such works are so much more dedicated to an idea than to life.

This is not to say that the novel is merely a mirror held up to life, as many have maintained, for successful ones clearly select and put into a meaningful order only certain elements of the totality of life. The novel is neither immoral nor amoral; it sets forth and defends values. In the case of individuations, however, these values are more often than not those of the dictates of the individual conscience as opposed to those of the dictates of society. This alignment of sympathies is not only a key to the early development of the novel form but precisely the source of Lukács' dissatisfaction with so much of European literature. He maintains that "later European realists," that is those writing after 1848, including Flaubert, Zola, and Maupassant, were mere observers of society, not champions of social progress; that their novels are filled with dead scenery and characters "of purely private interest" (*European Realism*, esp. pp. 143-145).

From an artistic point of view, it would be most difficult and perhaps even indefensible to argue that *War and Peace* is superior to *Madame Bovary*, or vice versa. The love that the socialist critics feel for Tolstoy is generated by two forces: the greatness of his art in terms of its execution and his rendering of Czarist society. If he had lived in the days of the Republic and had rendered that society in his work, he would have been viewed as a traitor, a counter-revolutionary, and the art of his work would have passed unnoticed. The novelist is moral, even dogmatic at times, but the author of individuations lashes out at the society portrayed which is usually the one in which he or she lives. Fortunately for his memory in Russia, Tolstoy repudiated the same society as the Revolution of 1910.

---

[34] Leo Tolstoi, Letter to Peter D. Boborykin, 1865, in *War and Peace*, trans. Louise and Aylmer Maude, ed. George Gibian, Norton Critical Edition (New York: W.W. Norton & Company, Inc., 1966), pp. 1359-1360.

Much of the morality of individuations stems from the fact that they stir the reader to self-recognition and evaluation, as well as a reevaluation of the surrounding world. The work may guide the reader, but this guidance develops or seems to develop as a natural course of the action. Normally individuation has done its work when it has exposed the problems, when it has asked the questions. It is not the author's job to provide solutions. Since in individuations self-scrutiny and the dialectical relationship between the individual and society is seen from the perspective of the character, he or she can grope toward a resolution that is satisfactory at least personally. Thus the mature Pip seems to have found peace with the world and values that are satisfactory from his point of view. Stephen Daedalus' decision to leave Ireland seems proper at the time, and the novel has surely persuaded many young readers that flight is the solution to their problems. Even Tolstoy's characters seem to reach some state of equilibrium that is satisfactory in their terms. Finally, novels of the eighteenth and nineteenth centuries, those that are termed "novels of manners," eventually reconcile the individual with society. This reconciliation is normally a result of change, and in these instances, more often than not, change on the part of the character more than on the part of his or her circumstances. In individuations the change is prepared for by the history of the conflict and is a result of growth rather than of sudden capitulation or an incredible stroke of fortune.

Individuation is a moral form because it not only provides an imitation of life but also supplies a perspective, one that begins with the author. It is impossible for the author to abandon the perspective, but it is ruinous to allow it to dominate the story. Just as individuation seeks a state of equilibrium between the character and the world, it also seeks to reconcile the author's view with reality. No matter how self-effacing an author may attempt to be, he or she creates the characters and their personalities, the physical world they inhabit, and the society in which they move. All are products of the author's own experience, and all must, to some degree, reflect his or her prejudices. The task is, in large part, not to allow vision to distort reality, but at the same time, to refuse to let reality destroy vision. Attempting to identify which of the characters in a novel represents the author has long been one of the favorite games played by readers and scholars. The entire content of a novel--all characters, all descriptions, all actions--are either direct manifestations or consequences of the author's perspective on life. The symbiotic relationship between author and text is frequently so complex that such issues can never be meaningfully resolved.

This concept of perspective is quite different from that held by Lukács, who maintains that the artist's perspective is manifested in a novel by the conclusion, the final and total vision, and that all other elements are selected and arranged to lead to that end.[35] While it is no doubt true that a great many novels were composed in that manner, it is also true that most of the worst examples were so composed, for in them we can readily observe the author forcing the characters and the action to move steadily toward the desired final statement or vision. Such is the case with the works of Frank Norris and legions of other social novelists. At times, as in the instance of *Doña Bárbara*, discussed in Chapter I, the action may get so far out of hand that extremely heavy-handed measures are required. Individuations are not written in this fashion, but are instead explorations of the interaction between a character with particular personality traits and social status and a particular surrounding environment. This method may result in an "arbitrary chronicle" (Lukács, p. 55) if the plot does not build on the basis of a causality resulting from interaction, but funneling the characters and action toward a final vision is potentially far more damaging to artistic quality.

Apparently, most individuations begin with an author's fascination with a specific character, or with a particular social milieu, or even with a desire to work out a particular personal or philosophical problem by giving it life and then following it until it reaches a solution. This is not to say that the author has no pre-conceived idea of where the story will lead, but that if it should happen to take a course not envisioned, he or she will be willing to follow. Such a work is an exploration and has a strong symbiotic relationship with its creator. Through it the artist can explore the consequences of specific personality traits and ideas much more fully and quickly than is possible in "real life." Thus in *Madame Bovary* Flaubert can cathartically work out his own conflicting romantic and realistic tendencies, and in *Death in Venice* Thomas Mann can attempt to resolve his dilemma of polarities between aesthetics versus reality, neoclassic control versus the romantic impulse. The reader is invited to accompany the author in such explorations. Just as the characters are created out of the author's psyche, the reader can recognize aspects of him or herself in them, and share in the author's cathartic experience.

----

[35]Georgy Lukács, "Franz Kafka or Thomas Mann?," in *The Meaning of Contemporary Realism*, p. 55.

The author and the reader thus meet and share vicariously the experience of the character. An individuation is a catalyst that through the characters blends, at least during the process of reading, the author, the reader, and a common perspective on society.

In such a relationship, the characters obviously have great importance, for they must captivate the attention and sympathy of the reader. Major novels are successful not because of what they reveal about societies, which may or may not stir the imagination of the reader, but because their characters are so appealing: "attention is turned to the personages themselves, not to their adventures. We are fascinated by Don Quixote and Sancho, not by what is happening to them."[36] This appeal of characters leads to a sense of sympathy and reader identification, even though the characters may not be individuals that we particularly admire or that we would wish to emulate. During the act of reading we temporarily give up at least a portion of our identity to share in part the identities of the characters with whom we empathize: "An 'other' becomes our temporary self" (Friedman, p. 13).

This process and the degree to which it is realized are naturally extremely complex issues. As Booth argues in his chapter on "The Morality of Impersonal Narration" (*Rhetoric of Fiction*, pp. 377-398), we are often confused as to whether we, as readers, should accept the views of the narrator or those of one of the characters, or whether any of these represents the views of the author. This sense of hesitation, however, reinforces the idea that the conflict in the work is critical. As in life we have difficulty in deciding where our natural sympathies lie, where they should lie, and where others (in this case the author) would have them lie:

> ... and as a rule if the novelist decides them one way or another it will ... be a sign that he has gone beyond his province, which is presentment, not explanation. He has done more than delineate, he has analysed and passed a

---

[36] José Ortega y Gasset, "The Dehumanization of Art," in *The Dehumanization of Art and Other Writings on Art and Culture*, trans. Willard Trask (Garden City: Doubleday & Company, Inc., 1956), p. 62.

judgment. He has made clear in his account what would not be clear in actual life . . . .[37]

Despite the natural reservations that a critical reader may have about accepting at face value the characters encountered in a novel, or about totally identifying with them, he or she will nonetheless, while reading, see the world from the perspective of one or more of the characters. As we begin to read we immediately begin to search for a central character, one with whom we can identify, one with whom we assume we are expected to identify. Later we may modify our loyalties or switch them entirely, but we are always either engaged sympathetically with a character or seeking such an engagement: "[A novel] obliges us in the first place to choose arbitrarily, but not injudiciously, one character as the center or focus of any event and to regard that character as the continuous inward center for the duration of any sequence of events" (Friedman, p. 12).

As we voluntarily submit ourselves to the perspective of a character, we offer, even though we may have reservations, our temporary sympathy. The very act of considering another's perspective is a sympathetic act. Booth insists on the need for the reader "to be with" a character. In describing Miranda ("Pale Horse, Pale Rider") he observes that "Very little heightening of her character is needed to make us unite with her against the hostile world around her" (*Rhetoric*, p. 276), and Watt sees reader sympathy as the key that distinguishes Moll Flanders from the traditional pícaro (*The Rise of the Novel*, p. 94). This is not to suggest that one and only one of the characters should gain our sympathy. We may find ourselves sharing the perspectives of several characters or not fully identifying with any single one: "The convincing texture of the whole, the impression of life as experienced by an observer, is in itself surely what the true artist seeks" (Booth, p. 346). Booth goes on to question who is the protagonist in *The Great Gatsby*. Is it Nick or is it Gatsby as seen by Nick? In "Heart of Darkness" is it Kurtz as seen by Marlow or is it Marlow as he experiences Kurtz? We are forced to agree that the question is meaningless. What matters is that we share in a perspective on society, on the world, or at least on one of its aspects.

---

[37]Wilfrid Philip Ward, "The Nature and Limits of a Character Study," in *Last Lectures by Wilfrid Ward* (Freeport, N.Y.: Books for Libraries Press, Inc., reprinted 1967), p. 153.

In many works the perspective we share is not so much that of one of the obvious characters as that of a narrator who may or may not have a physical presence in the work itself. In *Great Expectations*, we are caught in at least two perspectives--that of the young Pip, and that of the mature Pip who tells the story with a sense of irony that is subtle but that nonetheless controls our sympathy. Narrators are persons too, even when they remain hidden: "we react to all narrators as persons. We find their accounts credible or incredible, their opinions wise or foolish . . ." (Booth, p. 273). No matter what the perspective we share may be, it will surely be that of an individual, and because of the dialectical relationship between the individual and the society in which he or she lives, we are bound to sympathize to at least some degree with that individual and to share his or her discontent with all opposing forces. Individuations thus persuade us to be critical of social pressures and values: "By showing most of the story through Emma's eyes [Jane Austen] insures that we shall travel with Emma rather than stand against her" (Booth, p. 245). We may still be fully aware of Emma's faults, we may even dislike her, but because we share her perspective, we are forced to see her side and recognize any injustices committed against her.

Perhaps no work demonstrates more clearly how through merely accompanying a character the reader comes to sympathize with him or her than does *War and Peace*. As the separate portions of the story unfold we come to admire, feel compassion for, and deeply care for Mary Anatole Bolkonski. We admire her patience, her religious conviction and resignation, and regret her plight. Moreover, we are captivated by the charming and delightful Natasha Rostov. It is a shock for the reader when the two finally meet and openly detest one another. We care deeply for both, for we have seen the world from the perspective of each, but now, viewing both from without, we hardly recognize either character. In retrospect we may recognize that they were bound to conflict, but the scene of their first meeting is nonetheless painful.

Because of the combination of perspective and sympathy, the writer has a powerful hold on the reader, a hold quickly lost if we catch the author preaching, indoctrinating, or overtly attempting to manipulate our opinions. But the characters themselves, because they are convincing human beings and because we see life from their points of view, and above all, because the world so seen seems so convincing, so real, reader, character, and author unite against all forces that seek to control or destroy the life of the individual. No other form can begin to compete with individuations in terms of this threat to cultural proprieties. It is small wonder indeed that this type of novel is systematically banned in totalitarian states.

Before turning to the history of individualism and its effect on society and on literature, we must briefly consider one more type of authorial interference and its possible consequences: the imposition of form. The deliberate control of structure does not seem to be, potentially at least, so harmful as does overt manipulation of plot and character, although each has consequences affecting the other. Structure does not appear to be of major concern to the traditional realistic novelist: the life of the individual, or a segment of it, from birth to death or youth to marriage etc., provides the temporal limits, and the author has but to follow or pretend to follow that limited history. Later novelists, however, whether motivated by mere interest in experimenting with structure or, as in the case of writers dealing with torrents of psychic flow, forced to devise new structural methods as a defense against chaos, have carried (or followed) structure to extremes of complexity. Structure is harmful to individuations only if forced; if it is clear that the author valued structure more highly than mimesis. James Joyce in *Ulysses*, Alejo Carpentier in *El acoso (The Manhunt)*,[38] and a host of other twentieth-century novelists have proved that even the most ornate of preconceived structures can be wrought with no evidence of violence to the natural progression of a story. In most instances, however, preconceived structure seems to be more a general guide to the author than a blueprint:

> The prefigured structure of a novel seems less like the framework of pillars and arches which holds a building in a certain shape, than like the scaffolding, without which indeed the building cannot be started, but which is altered and dismantled in the process of construction.[39]

---

[38] Alejo Carpentier, *El acoso*, in *Guerra del tiempo* (México: Cía General de Ediciones, C.A., 1969), pp. 133-275.

[39] David Lodge, "Towards a Poetics of Fiction: An Approach Through Language," in *The Novelist at the Crossroads*, p. 58.

Structure seems most potentially harmful to individuations when it is most meaningful in terms of content: i.e., when it is a symbolic structure intended to set forth an ideology. The most abused of all is the circle, which time and again has been exploited to show the hopelessness of man's situation. As in action and in character, however, structure can be harmful only if forced, and again just as with action and character, structure cannot be dispensed with or ignored: "By its obligatory attention to the perceiving self, the flux of experience in the novel is also obliged to create (even against the novelist's will) an ethical form in process" (Friedman, p. 13). All aspects of content are aspects of organization, of structure:

> It is evident that a character is a verbal construction which has no existence outside the book. It is a vehicle for the novelist's sensibility and its significance lies in its relations with the author's other constructions. A novel is essentially a verbal pattern in which the different 'characters' are strands, and the reader's experience is the impact of the complete pattern on his sensibility.[40]

A major reason the novel had difficulty becoming accepted as a true art form is that it follows life rather than shaping it. Individuation is bound by the rules of experience and reality more strongly than by the rules of aesthetics and beauty. We are far more likely to forgive a writer for a flawed structure than we are to tolerate any departure from verisimilitude: "Who would exchange the flawed *Middlemarch* with its omissions made conspicuous by its suggestive reticence, for a novel where truth were reduced and mere aesthetic balance retained."[41] Structure then, despite its importance in the individuations, must take a back seat to the primary ingredients of the form: the individual in a dialectical relationship with the surrounding, threatening, and engulfing world. Interest in such a relationship is obviously impossible in a culture or a society that does not recognize the unique individual as a valuable entity. The novel did not appear in classical times because its most basic assumption was

---

[40]Martin Turnell, *The Novel in France* (New York: Vintage Books, 1958), p. 7.

[41]Barbara Hardy, *The Appropriate Form: An Essay on the Novel* (London: The Athlone Press, 1964), p. 131.

unthinkable. It does not thrive in historical periods of neo-classicism or under colonial conditions for precisely the same reason. It thrives or falters according to the esteem in which a society holds the individual human being, the subject of the next chapter.

CHAPTER THREE

Individualism and Individuation

In the modern world we have become so accustomed to the concept of individuality, to respecting and defending the rights of the individual, even when these stand against what may be best for the society in which that person functions, that we tend to forget that the very concept of individuality is a comparatively recent one, one that was long in coming and that has had many painful consequences. As recently as the Middle Ages the term "individual" meant "inseparable." Subsequently it came to denote a member of a group or of a class. About three hundred years ago, it came to mean simply "person" without reference to group or to class. Today's concept of a separate identity has evolved only since the early seventeenth century.[1] In all discussions but for those pertaining to mankind, to identify still means to recognize or determine the class to which a specimen belongs, while to identify a person is to recognize or determine his or her unique essence as distinct from all class or group ties. The history of the novel coincides closely with, and indeed depends heavily upon, the history of the concept of the individual as a separate essence with unique needs and rights.

In discussing the relationships that the individual may have with the society in which he or she exists, Raymond Williams divides persons into two broad categories: conforming and non-conforming, each with various levels or types. Among the conformists are members, subjects, and servants. The "member" fully belongs to society and accepts its values "to such an extent that he is proud to describe himself in its terms" (*Long Revolution*, p. 85). The "subject" does not fully belong and is not so pleased but suppresses personal desires for the sake of survival (p. 87). Finally, the "servant" feels less pressure than does the "subject" for the "servant" has the illusion of being able to choose. This illusion "allows him to pretend to an identification with the society, as if the choice had been real" (p. 87). Within the broad category of non-conformists, Williams finds rebels, exiles, and vagrants. The "rebel" is extremely rare, and like the conforming

---

[1]Raymond Williams, *The Long Revolution* (New York: Columbia University Press, 1961), pp. 73-74.

"member," has made a strong commitment to certain causes (p. 89). The social reformer and the social critic are not "rebels" but "members," for while they wish to improve society, they adhere to it in general. The "exile," like the "rebel," rejects society and its ways, but instead of fighting for a new order, escapes (p. 89). The "exile" need not physically abandon society, but may simply stay at home waiting for social changes that will make integration acceptable. The "vagrant" also stays home but drops out of society altogether, for lack of both pride and principle (p. 91). The "vagrant" may even enjoy great material success, for he or she is often capable of taking every advantage of circumstance. An individual may live his or her entire life as one of these six types, but is more likely to pass through two or more roles, and each implies a distinct perspective:

> To the member, society is his own community . . . . To the servant, society is an establishment, in which he finds his place. To the subject society is an imposed system, in which his place is determined. To the rebel, a particular society is a tyranny; the alternative for which he fights is a new and better society. To the exile, society is beyond him, but may change. To the vagrant, society is a name for other people, who are in his way or who can be used. (p. 92)

These perceptions seem at first glance to suggest that society is out to get the individual who must serve its ends or be destroyed or expelled. In fact, society, through family, friends, or out of a generally benevolent nature, may actually seek to help the individual, for conformity makes it easier for the individual to succeed, as Williams is quick to point out (p. 86).

In individuations, as in the life they seek to imitate, characters may assume any one or more of these six roles. Many of the protagonists of the great nineteenth century works are "members," for while they may seek to improve society, they are proud to be a part of it. This is especially true of many Victorian novels. The epic hero too is a "member," for his "destiny connects him by indissoluble threads to the community whose fate is crystallised in his own."[2] At the opposite

----

[2]Georgy Lukács, *The Theory of the Novel*, trans. Anna Bostock (Cambridge Mass.: The MIT Press, 1971), p. 67.

end of the spectrum, at the extreme end of the non-conformers, is the "vagrant" who has been immortalized time and again in the picaresque tale. Recently the vagrant staged a comeback in the works of Beckett, Sartre, etc., as the natural hero of existentialism and of the absurd. At the upper end of the non-conformists is the "rebel," who would seem a likely candidate for the hero of individuations, but who is extremely rare. Rebels are more akin to the heroes of Byron or Espronceda in that they may go into physical exile, but seek to establish a new order with new values. They are more typical of the epic, if they succeed, or of romance. The others, the "subject," the "servant," the "exile," are all well-represented in individuations. They struggle, wait, hope, and complain. The "subjects" and "servants" are generally seeking to become "members," while the "exiles" are hoping for better days and better circumstances, or reminiscing about "the good old days" when they or their ancestors were either "members" or "rebels." Don Quixote wants to be, strives to be a "rebel," but his adventures tend to drive him back into the role of "exile," and ultimately make of him a "member." Julien Sorel would be a "member" but his circumstances contrive to make him now a "subject," now a "servant." The history of Hans Castorp is one of an apathetic "exile" who matures into a "member." Only the pure "member," one who is neither a reformer nor a critic, would seem to be antithetical to individuations. What is most typical is an individual who passes through more than one of these roles, and who is constantly struggling to find a different, more satisfying place in society.

These general categories of individual/societal relationships all clearly have one thing in common: the concept that each human being is in a sense separate, or at least potentially separable from other human beings, not only as a physical entity but as a psychological entity as well. Erich Fromm believes that human beings are distinguished by the fact that they must make intellectual choices rather than be guided purely by instinct. Choice implies freedom, but it is not "freedom to" but rather "freedom from instinctual determination of his actions."[3] Fromm sees eating from the tree of knowledge as the first human act, for even though organized religion sees it as the original sin, it represents the first step toward freedom, toward being human (p. 34). This act was a critical first step toward "individua-

---

[3] Erich Fromm, *Escape from Freedom* (New York: Holt, Rinehart and Winston, 1941), p. 32.

tion," a process that embodies both positive and negative consequences.

Individuation is a two-edged sword. Societal ties impede the total emergence of an individual, yet provide protection. On the one hand, the community blocks freedom and development; on the other, it provides security: "He belongs to, he is rooted in, a structuralized whole in which he has an unquestionable place. He may suffer from hunger or suppression, but he does not suffer from the worst of all pains--complete aloneness and doubt" (p. 35). Fromm has just described at least two of the categories of Williams: the subject and the exile, both common in the novel. Individuations have recorded more fully than any other form the agony of this conflict between the desire for freedom and the need for security. Indeed, many of the greatest novels are based on the struggle between these irreconcilable poles.

In classical times this confrontation was not allowed to take place, at least not in the cases of epic heroes. Piety--*pietas*--pledged the individual firstly to the will of the Gods and secondly to the State. If there was room for additional dutifulness, then it was accorded to the family. Aeneas and Odysseus were pious, Dido was not, nor would Achilles seem to have been. But as Hegel points out, even though heroic action may seem to be motivated by individual desires, individuality in such cases exists in a sort of social vacuum:

> The Romans already had their city and their legal institutions, and, in contrast to the state as the universal end, personality had to be sacrificed. To be just a Roman ... this is the seriousness and dignity of Roman virtue. Heroes, on the other hand, are individuals who undertake and accomplish the entirety of an action, actuated by the independence of their character and caprice; and in their case, therefore, it appears as the effect of individual disposition when they carry out what is right and moral. But this immediate unity of the substantial with the individuality of inclination, impulses, and will is inherent in Greek virtue, so that individuality is a law to itself, without being subjected to an independently subsisting law, judgement, and tribunal.[4]

---

[4]G.W.F. Hegel, *Aesthetics*, trans. T.M. Knox (Oxford: Oxford University

Epic heroes, then, are not individuals in any modern sense. Throughout antiquity virtuous characters upheld the values of religion and state, that is, the values established and defended by society. Those characters who did not were comic, not heroic: "their relation to the social whole is either a matter of clever adaptation or of grotesquely blameworth isolation. In the latter case, the realistically portrayed individual is always in the wrong in his conflict with the social whole . . . ."[5] In more modern times, and particularly in individuations, society may be equally or more blameworthy for any schism that isolates the individual.

The great advantage to literature in the classical point of view was that the artist was not compelled to serve as mediator between the individual and society: "the individual as such does not yet in those days find the substantial, the moral, the right, contrasted with himself as necessitated by law, and thus far the poet is immediately confronted with what the Ideal demands" (Hegel, I, p. 190). So long as this state of affairs endured, there was no opportunity for individuations, even though many scholars trace the novel's roots to the early comic narratives in which the individual was entirely to blame for all personal problems. In Western literature, individuation is more clearly traceable to Judeo-Christian tradition, for while the Pentateuch certainly does not exalt the individual as opposed to the group, it reflects a far greater complexity of issues than the Homeric tales (Auerbach, p. 20). We also find a greater awareness of individual/social relations in Icelandic sagas than in Homer, as Scholes and Kellogg point out.[6] The combination of these major influences on Western literature is at least partially responsible for the emergence of the hero we associate with individuation. The literary precedents are, of course, many, but before individuations are possible, the person must be more than just a personality: the individual must reach parity with society, a process that required hundreds of years.

Press, 1975), Vol. I, p. 185.

[5] Erich Auerbach, *Mimesis: The Representation of Reality in Western Literature*, trans. Willard R. Trask (Princeton: Princeton University Press, 1968), p. 31.

[6] Robert Scholes and Robert Kellogg, *The Nature of Narrative* (London, Oxford, New York: Oxford University Press, 1968), p. 174.

Today's concept of individualism is thus quite recent. The term itself was coined in France (*individualisme*) during the early nineteenth century.[7] It was applied vigorously in a pejorative sense by critics of the Enlightenment, and its negative connotations have survived in France to this day. In Germany, *Individualität* was a romantic concept glorifying the value of the individual as opposed to the abstract systematizations of the Enlightenment. In England, nineteenth century thinkers such as John Stewart Mill associated individualism with the evils of capitalism and economic competition. Only in the United States has individualism come to be fully glorified as an ideology of freedom and justice, as the last and greatest stage of human evolution. Even though the term grew out of reactions against the Enlightenment, with negative connotations in France and England and positive connotations in Germany and the United States, the concept and its sociological reality are traceable to antiquity. One of the most decisive factors was the dawn of Christianity and the New Testament idea that each person is important; that God cares about the individual, not just the nation.

Aristotle first advanced the idea of the autonomy of the individual, but the concept was relatively unimportant until the thirteenth century when Saint Thomas Aquinas argued that the individual conscience should be given supremacy even over direct orders from superiors; that the individual has a direct relationship with God that must not be violated, even by the Church. The evolution of this concept played a critical role in the eventual development of the novel form, as Ian Watt observes.[8] Despite the arguments of Aquinas, however, the Roman Catholic Church continued to stress the need to sacrifice the individual for the good of the social whole: "*Utilitas publica prefertur utilitati privatae*" (Lukes, p. 597). After the next major step, taken under the leadership of Calvin and Luther, esteem for the individual grew rapidly. However, the Reformation also gave rise to

---

[7]For a history of the term and for many skeletal concepts used in the following discussion of the growth of individualism, I am greatly indebted to Stephen Lukes' "Types of Individualism," in the *Dictionary of the History of Ideas: Studies of Selected Pivotal Ideas*, ed. Philip P. Wiener (New York: Charles Scribner's Sons, 1973), Vol. II, pp. 594-601. Further credit is given only in the case of direct quotations.

[8]Ian Watt, *The Rise of the Novel: Studies in Defoe, Richardson and Fielding* (Berkeley and Los Angeles: University of California Press, 1967), p. 14.

an emphasis on the wickedness and insignificance of the individual. These opposed attitudes are reflected in the positions of Protestantism and Catholicism (Fromm, pp. 38-39). The Reformation thus contained the seeds of the conflict that is central to individuations: on the one hand individual freedom and autonomy; on the other, individual insignificance and weakness and a need to subordinate oneself to a higher power. While Kant brought the concept of individual freedom and autonomy to the stage most typified in individuations, Spinoza and Locke, in the seventeenth century, had already refined it. As Watt suggests, their new orientations were key in the development of the novel (p. 62). With these philosophical developments the stage was nearly set for the sudden flourishing of individuations. But along with moral, political and social emancipation came certain additional freedoms, all, of course, at a price.

Primary among the corollaries to individualism are self-development and economic independence. Self-development may be traced at least as far as the Italian Renaissance, and was a key ingredient of romanticism. Economic individualism was not fully worked out until about the middle of the eighteenth century, even though its roots are traceable to the beginnings of the Renaissance and the breakdown of feudalism. Even in their earliest forms, these concepts fostered a new freedom: "capitalistic economy put the individual entirely on his own feet" (Fromm, p. 108). This freedom for self-development, this social independence, and this concept of the individual as separate from any group, are quite in contrast to the views of Antiquity and even of the Middle Ages:

> Neither does the heroic individual separate himself from the ethical whole to which he belongs; on the contrary, he has a consciousness of himself only as in substantial unity with this whole. *We* on the other hand, according to our views nowadays, separate ourselves, as persons with our personal aims and relationships, from the aims of such a community . . . . (Hegel, I, p. 188)

The apogee of the free individual is to be found in capitalism, and in the rise of the bourgeoisie: "it becomes evident that the man who now emerges must be the individual, egoistic bourgeois isolated artificially by capitalism and that his consciousness, the source of his activity and knowledge, is an individual isolated consciousness à la Robinson Crusoe."[9] This view, totally opposed to that held by the societies that produced the great epics, demanded a new literary form for its expression. The novel, particularly the individuation, is, then, the typical expression of capitalistic society which fosters personal freedom.

Such freedom comes at a great price, however. There is, of course, the price paid for failure in capitalistic economies, examples of which fill novels in the nineteenth and twentieth centuries. The themes of exploitation and greed are as old as the genre itself. Success too has a cost. The great characters of individuations have one thing in common, be they economic successes or abject failures, they are isolated. In short, they are faithful imitations of modern man:

> The individual is freed *from* the bondage of economic and political ties. He also gains in positive freedom by the active and independent role which he has to play in the new system. But simultaneously he is freed from those ties which used to give him security and a feeling of belonging . . . he is alone, isolated, threatened from all sides. (Fromm, p. 62)

Individuations fully and deliberately explore this ambiguous freedom as characters struggle to reconcile its opposite poles; i.e. to be free only in the positive sense, without the price of isolation and insecurity.

As all of these cultural factors--philosophical, sociological, and economic--were sliding into place to set the stage for the great boom of the novel in the nineteenth century, Hegel was publishing his comprehensive philosophy and advancing his theory of the dialectical history of the universe. The conflict that is central to individuations exemplifies the dialectical model, and has a strong economic emphasis as well. Economics plays a vital role in novels; it is difficult to imagine a novel without strong economic concerns. Even Robinson Crusoe is obsessed with the accumulation and cataloguing of wealth. There is, in fact, a vital relationship between the novel form and the change to an economy based on exchange value rather than use value: "There

---

[9] Georgy Lukács, "Reification and the Consciousness of the Proletariat," in *History and Class Consciousness: Studies in Marxist Dialectics*, trans. Rodney Livingstone (Cambridge Mass.: The MIT Press, 1971), p. 135.

is a *rigorous homology* between the literary form of the novel . . . and the everyday relation between man and commodities in general, and by extension between man and other men, in a market society."[10] A major reason for the socialist critics' love of the novel form is that it exposes and exploits this "unhealthy" economic situation that is clearly a product of rising capitalism. Lukács in particular stresses the significance of market society and the corresponding isolation of the individual: "It is not men's consciousness that determines their existence, but on the contrary, their social existence that determines their consciousness."[11] Lukács, who demands that conflict be used to improve the social situation ("for the dialectical method the central problem *is to change reality*"--"Orthodox Marxism," p. 3), will not tolerate the theory, advanced by Max Adler, that the conflict is simply one of the individual against society:

> By this stroke the objective economic antagonism as expressed in the *class struggle* evaporates, leaving only a conflict between the *individual* and *society*. This means that neither the emergence of internal problems, nor the collapse of capitalist society, can be seen as necessary. ("Orthodox Marxism," p. 11)

This view of the conflict, and a corresponding desire to see conflict in literature take the form of a class struggle, has resulted in socialist countries in individuation all but disappearing as a viable art form. As we have seen, such missionary tasks are better accomplished through the epic or other genres.

Individuation is the literary expression not of the proletarian revolution, but of the Industrial Revolution, which provided not only a philosophical base but the practical wherewithal for it to flourish. Ian Watt and Raymond Williams have documented the significance of the Industrial Revolution for the rise of the novel in England, but it is important to remember that the other independent nation most affected by the Revolution was France, and that these two countries were the cradles of the golden age of the novel, the nineteenth cen-

----

[10]Lucien Goldmann, *Towards a Sociology of the Novel*, trans. Alan Sheridan (London: Tavistock Publications Limited, 1975), p. 7.

[11]Georgy Lukács, "What is Orthodox Marxism," in *History and Class Consciousness*, p. 18.

tury.[12] The first and perhaps most significant impact of the Industrial Revolution on the novel, even more important than the technology it provided for the mechanical production of literature at a reasonable price, the rise of a readership, and the other factors stressed by Watt and Williams, was the rise of the middle class and the inseparable enthusiasm for individualism:

> "Bourgeois" is a significant term because it marks that version of social relationship which we usually call individualism: that is to say, an idea of society as a neutral area within which each individual is free to pursue his own development and his own advantage as a natural right. The course of recent history is marked by a long fighting retreat from this idea in its purest form, and the latest defenders would seem to the earliest to have lost almost the entire field. Yet the interpretation is still dominant: the exertion of social power is thought necessary only in so far as it will protect individuals in this basic right to set their own course. (Williams, *Culture and Society*, p. 312)

It is the setting of one's own course, or at least the attempt to do so, that we find at the heart of virtually all individuations.

Goldmann makes an extremely important contribution to the understanding of the nature of conflict in individuations by outlining four factors that lead to the creation of the novel and in explaining the appearance of what he terms the "problematic individual." The first is the sudden significance of exchange value as opposed to use value; i.e. the importance of money, "together with a propensity to make of money and social prestige absolute values and not merely mediations that provide access to other values . . . ." The second is the presence of "individuals who are essentially *problematic* in so far as their thinking and behaviour remain dominated by qualitative values." These include, among others, philosophers and writers. Thirdly, and perhaps most importantly for our purposes, there was a rising dissatisfaction with the lack of qualitative values "either in society as a whole, or perhaps solely among the middle strata from which most novelists have come." Thus the novel was born from a

----

[12]Watt, *Rise of the Novel*, Raymond Williams, *Culture and Society 1780-1950* (Harmondsworth, Middlesex: Penguin Books Ltd., 1961), and *The Long Revolution*.

need to express what Goldmann calls "affective discontent." Finally, he stresses the significance of liberal individualism, rendered and defended in the novel through the biographies of individuals. Creative writers who were in themselves problematic, at odds with the quantitative value system of their time, used their own experiences and observations as the basis for the conflicts we find in their novels, which express "the internal contradiction between individualism as a universal value produced by bourgeois society and the important and painful limitations that this society itself brought to the possibilities of the development of the individual."[13]

This major conflict between types of values received great impetus from the rise of romanticism and its exaltation of the individual. Almost simultaneously, the two major countries of the new industrial age, France and England, found themselves torn by major social upheavals that stemmed directly from the fact that they were not equipped to deal with and accomodate the burgeoning new class. The impact of the French Revolution is more obvious, but as Carlyle observed, "These Chartisms, Radicalisms, Reform Bill, Tithe Bill, and infinite other discrepancy, and acrid argument and jargon that there is yet to be, are *our* French Revolution: God grant that we, with our better methods, may be able to transact it by argument alone."[14]

If we leave sociological and economic factors aside, which we cannot legitimately do, the literary father of the novel, the movement that gave it birth, is romanticism. But the major trait of individuation is realism, which, like romanticism, is closely associated with liberal forces: "If the case for realism has any ideological content it is that of liberalism."[15] While realism is often viewed, legitimately, as a reaction against romanticism, particularly against its sentimental excesses, it in fact sustains and advances the ideals of liberalism and individualism, as Auerbach has argued (*Mimesis*, pp. 473-474). Even though Auerbach has traced the threads of realism back to antiquity,

----

[13]All quotes come from Goldmann, *Sociology of the Novel*, p. 11 and p. 12.
[14]Thomas Carlyle, *Carlyle: Selected Works, Reminiscences and Letters*, ed. Julian Symons (Cambridge, Mass.: Harvard University Press, 1970), p. 275. This quote is from Carlyle's essay *Chartism*, Chapter Five, "Rights and Mights."
[15]David Lodge, "The Novelist at the Crossroads," in *The Novelist at the Crossroads and Other Essays on Fiction and Criticism* (Ithaca: Cornell University Press, 1971), p. 33.

one aspect of the novel that is "novel" is its concern for these "characters of any station" and the "practical everyday complications of their lives" as serious subjects for literature.

No other literary form is sufficiently amorphous to perform this task. Since the subject and its treatment are the bases for the modern concept of realism, and since the novel was the one form ideally suited for such treatment, the novel and realism have been historically linked, and Auerbach has pointed out that both have had their greatest success in France and in England (p. 491). Auerbach, of course, is not so concerned with the novel as he is with realism. Because of his focus, he is not overly interested in individualism or in the nature of the conflict we find in individuations. Williams, on the other hand, views realism as the embodiment of relationships between individuals and their societies: "society is seen in fundamentally personal terms, and persons, through relationships, in fundamentally social terms" (*Long Revolution*, p. 287). This view is shared by Harry Levin, who points to its embodiment in French literature: "French literature has been preoccupied, not so much with the individual in isolation or with society in the mass, as with the problem of keeping the balance between them."[16]

Auerbach, Williams, and Levin would seem to agree that the reality of realism is social. The idyllic marvels of romanticism have been left behind as literature turns its attention to society, generally urban. Once again, capitalism is a major factor in this development, for it not only created the new class but brought its members together. Lukács even argues that only the advent of capitalism made it possible to view society as reality in the first place ("Orthodox Marxism," p. 19). Capitalism, moreover, with its emphasis on individualism and self-development, brought with it a new time perspective, a focus on the future rather than on the past. This perspective distinguishes not only eighteenth and nineteenth century

---

[16] Harry Levin, "Realism in Perspective," in *Approaches to the Novel: Materials for a Poetics*, ed. Robert Scholes, rev. ed. (San Francisco: Chandler Publishing Co., 1966), pp. 112-113.

society from predecessors, but individuation from its most important ancestor, the epic:

> As opposed to all preceding formations which were oriented towards the past, capitalism is oriented towards the future as a result of the "infinite process" of capitalist production. This orientation towards the future is the initial tendency of the novel, and it is matched by the activity in which the hero constitutes his own world. In the epic, not only is the universe's general framework determined from the outset by the will of the Olympians, but so is action: the hero will only accomplish the task that has been *assigned* him.[17]

The conflict of individuations moves forward in time as the character goes about the task of constituting a personal world, a process that is impossible until the individual achieves prized status.

The struggle between the individual and environmental restrictions takes many forms. The dramatic social upheavals that took place from the Reformation on left no aspect of life unaffected. As Williams points out, the genre was not concerned only with the clash between country life and city life, the old way versus the new, agriculture versus industry, and so on down the line, but also it explored the tension between customs and education, the tension that acted on each individual who was torn between a natural heritage--language, mannerisms, dress, etc.--and those values that were taught as "proper." Properness was the key to advancement, to improvement of one's station in life, yet the individual may wish to maintain ties to the inherited stratum, to friends and family.[18] Clearly such is not always the case, but this type of conflict reveals just how complex and how numerous were the possibilities of the novel form, and we can find this complexity in the major individuations of all cultures.

In all such instances, focus is on the individual as a unique essence, not as a representative of a class or a concept. Each case is therefore unique, "and interest in such a figure . . . is unendingly par-

---

[17] Ferenc Fehér, "Is the Novel Problematic? A Contribution to the Theory of the Novel," *Telos*, 15 (1973), p. 51.

[18] Raymond Williams, *The English Novel from Dickens to Lawrence* (New York: Oxford University Press, 1970).

ticular" (Hegel, I, p. 194). Nonetheless, the author of an individuation cannot sacrifice society to the demands of the individual, as did Ibsen:

> Ibsen owed his European fame to the social message of his plays, which was reducible, in the final analysis, to a single idea, the duty of the individual towards himself, the task of self-realization, the enforcement of one's own nature against the narrow-minded, stupid and out-of-date conventions of society.[19]

In fact individuation cannot lean very far in either direction without disappearing. If a work becomes so concerned with the individual that society disappears, at least in terms of positive values, we are left with the picaresque, or satire, or a sort of romantic manifesto; if the individual is sacrificed we are left with epic. When in modern societies the balance is disturbed, when society comes to be viewed as more important than its individual members, and when its members agree with that principle, either voluntarily or involuntarily, individuations disappear. This has been a common phenomenon in the twentieth century.

There are many compelling reasons for the retreat from individualism. Fromm has pointed out a number of major psychological factors: the terrible loneliness of the liberated individual, the lack of direction and purpose in life that such a person feels. Significantly, he entitled his book *Escape* **From** *Freedom*. Moreover, twentieth century politics have striven to make fragmented society whole again either by new ideologies or through coercion. Totalitarianism, whether its perspective be from the right or the left of the ideological spectrum, offers the individual, in exchange for liberty, a system, a sense of belonging, security, direction, and purpose. Whole nations have found this exchange acceptable.

The detrimental effect of fascism on literature is well known. Individualism and social criticism, which serve as the base of individuations, were impossible under the governments of Hitler and Mussolini, and we can find numerous examples that are equally illustrative

---

[19]Arnold Hauser, *The Social History of Art* (New York: Alfred A. Knopf, 1952), p. 916.

in the abundant right wing dictatorships of the Third World. Franco's Spain was slightly less rigid, probably because it had to be to survive in its time, but scores of Spanish artists were either jailed or went into exile, or both, and Spain, which could boast of a number of major artists, including novelists, before the Civil War, produced no individuation of major international significance after Franco gained full power. The few good novelists who managed to publish individuations used as major themes pre-Franco days (Carmen Laforet), the ignorance of rural society (Cela), ennui (Sánchez Ferlioso), or other relatively safe topics. Works that were critical of the mainstream of Spanish society, such as Martín Santos' *Tiempo de silencio*, are rare and therefore doubly significant.

While considerable attention has been paid to the novel and fascism, the detrimental effects of socialism on the genre have been relatively ignored. This is no doubt partially a result of the quality and the quantity of socialist criticism and theory on the novel, and may also be due to the fact that many of the greatest Russian writers have been novelists. Socialism, like right wing fascism, came about in part as a reaction to and a breakwater against rampant individualism which threatened to destroy many societies. Socialism once again values society above the individual: "Socialist equality in contrast [to bourgeois equality] demands that individual achievement is not gained at the expense of others and to the detriment of community."[20] The defenders of socialism, however, are not willing to accept, at least openly, the sacrifice of the individual for the communal good. Instead they attempt to redefine the meaning of individuality. Thus Trotsky argues that "Individuality is a welding together of tribal, national, class, temporary and institutional elements and, in fact, it is in the uniqueness of this welding together, in the proportions of this psychochemical mixture, that individuality is expressed."[21] There is, then, an attempt on the part of socialist thinkers to define the individual as an integral part of the social whole rather than as an entity separate from that whole. This new definition and concept of the individual virtually destroys the "problematic individual," the hero of individuations.

---

[20] Alan Swingewood, *The Novel and Revolution* (Great Britain: Barnes & Noble, 1975), p. 55.
[21] Leon Trotsky, *Literature and Revolution*, trans. Rose Strunsky (Ann Arbor: University of Michigan Press, 1960), p. 60.

Balzac and the other novelists applauded in socialist criticism attacked bourgeois society through their problematic heroes. But they did not attack that society merely because they considered it a great evil; they attacked it because it formed their own social realities. Once reality has become socialist, the novelist has great difficulty in practicing his art, for individuation becomes impossible. Dissension over the novelist's role has characterized the Soviet literary scene: "critics argued that proletarian literature should not concern itself with the 'inner life of heroes', or give prominence to sex and the unconscious: its role must be bound up with the immediate problems of socialist reconstruction" (Swingewood, p. 99). This line of argument, typical of socialist governments with strong central control, clearly destroys the possibility of individuation as a viable art form by denying social dissidence, the "everlasting no" of the novelist. The political reality of socialism is that it merely replaces the epic tenet that the desires of the individual must be subservient to the needs of the nation (essentially the aristocracy) with the tenet that they must be subservient to the needs of the class (essentially the proletariat). In capitalism, the individual fights for personal interests and is not faulted for it, for everyone else is doing the same. Fault is found only if the individual destroys others through private greed, as is the case of the daughters of Père Goriot. Individuals' struggles to reconcile gain with conscience, personal desires with social and moral codes, provide the plots for individuations.

Social evolution has conspired against individualism and against its literary champion. Bourgeois society rose because of industrialism, but industry also brought together the working masses and formed a new social order that because of its vast size was destined to challenge for power. And, since the power of the proletariat lies not in its wealth but in its size, it had to become social to be effective, and this socialization is precisely its history: "Working-class culture, in the stage through which it has been passing, is primarily social (in that it has created institutions) rather than individual (in particular intellectual or imaginative work)" (Williams, *Culture and Society*, p. 314).

Moreover, extraordinary personal freedom has proven less than thrilling, for the severance of primary bonds has not been compensated for by the creation of new ties of security. Freedom becomes a burden which individuals feel pressured to give up in order to gain relief from doubt and uncertainty (Fromm, pp. 36-37). As Fromm goes on to argue, it is not that we gained too much freedom, too much individualism, but that "what we believe to be individualism has become an empty shell" (p. 270). Fromm believes full freedom can be achieved only in a society which has as its goal the growth and happiness of each individual, and which does not require that that individual be "manipulated by any power outside of himself" (pp. 270-271). We are far from such a utopian state, and in many societies citizens are finding it preferable to relinquish some individual freedom in exchange for greater security.

The seeming failure of individualism is in part a result of the economic and sociological changes that have grown out of capitalism, changes that conspire against individualism itself. The "reification" of man, a process Goldmann claims has been at work for centuries, has resulted from the development of large trusts and monopolies which in turn squeeze out and destroy the individual capitalist. Marxists describe this process as a change from liberal capitalism to economic imperialism. The individual is now subservient to the corporation, and in a subsequent development, since World War II, governments have begun to intervene in the economy, removing the individual one step further from self-determination (*Sociology of the Novel*, pp. 135-136). If Goldmann's arguments are as valid as they seem, then once more the individual is subservient to structure, and society may have traced the full circle Frye observes in the history of literary modes.[22] Contemporary society attempts to bring the individual back into the fold: "Society penetrates the individual claiming that he cannot survive the terrors of the self without the protective blanket of societal rituals and institutions. Our religions, our myths, our taboos, our mores, all reflect it."[23] In many countries, including the United States, which is experiencing an unprecedented boom in conservative religious fervor, the individual would seem to be accepting this security.

Amidst the retreats from freedom that apparently characterize the contemporary world, there are those who have argued vociferously for a return to the hero:

---

[22] Northrop Frye, *Anatomy of Criticism: Four Essays* (New York: Atheneum, 1967), p. 42.
[23] Jerzy Kosinski, in *The New Fiction: Interviews with Innovative American Writers*, ed. Joe David Bellamy (Chicago: University of Illinois Press, 1974), p. 167.

> It is not society that is to guide and save the creative hero, but precisely the reverse. And so every one of us shares the supreme ordeal--carries the cross of the redeemer--not in the bright moments of his tribe's great victories, but in the silences of his personal despair.[24]

The hero for whom Campbell calls is not, clearly, the hero of individuations. It is not the problematic, rather ordinary human being who seeks but to reach a satisfactory state of equilibrium between personal needs and desires and that which society accords. Campbell's hero is a leader of men, of the tribe, of society; in short the hero of the epic. And, in fact, epic literature is becoming more and more common, as are its counterparts, satire and the picaresque. Theatre has in many ways become the defender of the individual, perhaps because it can portray the conflict more intensely, with less distraction. The modern tragic hero is in conflict with the moral laws of society, and is not a victim of a great universal pattern as were the classical tragic heroes: "the heroism lies in the rebellion, and is vindicated even in defeat" (Williams, *Long Revolution*, p. 267). This does not mean that drama has become a substitute for individuation. The hero of social tragedy is more single-dimensional, the lines of conflict more sharply drawn, the conflict itself more illustrative than representational. Moreover, we must observe that in a society that is not amenable to criticism from individuals it is apparently easier to write and perform theatre than to publish individuations. The novel continues to be contingent on economic factors. It is expensive to produce; it requires a vast readership to survive. It is thus more easily censored and suppressed.

The retreat from individualism, the rapid advancement of technology, and the progressive polarization of societies, with capitalism becoming increasingly conservative and liberalism increasingly socialistic, with neither extreme conducive to novelistic activity, do not harbinger the death of individuation. As we shall see in Chapter Five, the circumstances that make this literary form possible are reproducible in many societies, and in fact seem to characterize a stage through which all developing societies pass, even if only briefly. Indeed, while critics are grieving (or celebrating) the death of the traditional novel

----

[24]Joseph Campbell, *The Hero with a Thousand Faces* (Cleveland: World Publishing Company, 1956), p. 391.

in Europe and the United States, it is thriving, often in startling new forms, in other areas of the world. Now, however, we must examine the dissident nature of the individuation.

CHAPTER FOUR

The Novel as Dissent

Even though individuations are particularly modern, products of the radical cultural changes that swept the Western world from the seventeenth century on and culminating in the late eighteenth and early nineteenth, there are isolated examples long before the Industrial Revolution. One of the earliest is *Don Quixote*, which antedates even Descartes' thesis that knowledge begins with the individual. Such idiosyncratic works do not form a tradition, however, and are to a large degree products of historical accidents, in the case of *Don Quixote* the peculiar cultural characteristics of Spain at the beginning of the seventeenth century. By mid-century, to write an individuation would have been impossible.

The early novel was not just "novel," it was revolutionary. It defended and championed the cause of the new liberalism, and in particular of individualism. It shared with romanticism enthusiasm for such causes, but departed from that movement in that it did not idealize them. Individuation has been throughout its history practical, objective, and "realistic" in its rendering of the individual and the world. Because of this allegiance, each new character provides a new perspective, and each story determines its own form. The novel's "primary criterion was truth to individual experience--individual experience which is always unique and therefore new."[1] The novelist, merely by practicing his or her art, is therefore not only a social dissident, but a literary innovator as well. The key to this critical perspective, as we have argued, is the character, rendered as a real-life human being, facing real-life human problems, poised against the world. But this world is not of necessity evil. Individuation champions individualism through sympathetic portrayal; it seldom calls for the total destruction of opposing forces. It is the balance that concerns the artist: sympathy and understanding for the individual who craves freedom and the power of self-determination on the one hand; on the other the preservation, though perhaps modification of civilization. On the one hand individual freedom, on the other security. On

---

[1] Ian Watt, *The Rise of the Novel: Studies in Defoe, Richardson and Fielding* (Berkeley and Los Angeles: University of California Press, 1967), p. 13.

the one hand social tolerance and understanding, on the other preservation of moral and social canons.

Individuations bring these opposing interests together in an attempt to reconcile their claims:

> The main lesson of Auerbach's *Mimesis* ... is that the great realistic narratives combine the tragic concern for the individual with the comic concern for society to produce a representation of reality which is a just reflection of actual conditions and at the same time displays a tragic and problematic concern for the individual, regardless of his place in the social hierarchy.[2]

As we have seen, however, author and reader sympathy tend naturally to gravitate toward the character, from whose perspective the world is generally seen and whose problems seem so like ours. "We," of course, are the middle class, the primary beneficiaries and victims of individualism. "Our" problems are those that we meet every day, and our first line of defense was Samuel Richardson, "the first to make the new middle-class man, with his private life, living within the framework of the home, absorbed by his family affairs, unconcerned with fictitious adventures and marvels, the centre of a literary work."[3] Later novelists turned their attention to men and women from increasingly lower on the social and economic scale, but their concerns and sympathies for the people they portrayed remained unchanged. Only when novelists began to believe that the solution to man's problems lies in unity, in organization, in giving up some of the freedom gained in past centuries in exchange for security and the promise of a better life, did individuation fall on hard times.

From the outset, then, the novelist championed the individual, and early novels reflected a new way of looking at the individual and at the world. Of paramount importance in this change was woman: woman as an individual essence, equal in importance to the male, woman as an artist, and perhaps even more significant, the female

---

[2] Robert Scholes and Robert Kellogg, *The Nature of Narrative* (London, Oxford, New York: Oxford University Press, 1968), p. 229.

[3] Arnold Hauser, *The Social History of Art* (New York: Alfred A. Knopf, 1952), p. 562.

perspective. If it were possible to determine the sex of literary genres, the epic would surely be masculine, individuation feminine. The typical male interests at the time of the rise of the novel centered around action--hunting, gaming, etc.--and men's reading, if they read at all, centered around politics, business, adventure, sport, and so forth. Richardson again was in the vanguard by turning focus from external action to internal, psychological concerns, a point made by Watt (p. 244). Richardson placed utmost importance on what were typically viewed as feminine concerns. The male attitude seems to have been to judge a person by deeds, by accomplishments. Women were more interested in thoughts, feelings, the moral quality of the individual. Richardson's concern with psychology, the subjective world of his characters, and the new sexual ideology caused his contemporaries to refer to him as an old woman. His female characters are virtuous, but victims of male domination. He was deeply concerned with pleasing the new female readership, and his sensibility was in many ways feminine.

The feminine perspective for the novel has never received adequate attention, and while it is surely no accident that women are to be found not only among the earliest novelists of most countries but also among the greatest, many of the issues taken up by the novel, even though they seem to have preoccupied women first, are of vital interest to both sexes and receive full and just treatment from male authors as well. In England, for example, women have played a vital role in the history of the novel, as authors, subjects, and readers. They formed one of the new major powers in England during and after the Industrial Revolution, as Raymond Williams observes.[4] Ian Watt argues that the significance of Jane Austen "suggests that the feminine sensibility was in some ways better equipped to reveal the intricacies of personal relationships and was therefore at a real advantage in the realm of the novel" (*Rise of the Novel*, p. 298). Long after Austen, Dorothy Richardson would complain that male novelists had too much action, and not enough reverie, feeling, and perceiving.[5] Moreover, one of the virtues of Anthony Trollope that was not wasted on Henry James was his" feminine" sensibility:

---

[4]Raymond Williams, *The Long Revolution* (New York: Columbia University Press, 1961), p. 240.

[5]Leon Edel, *The Modern Psychological Novel* (New York: Grove Press and Evergreen Books, 1955), pp. 73-74.

> His great, his inestimable merit was a complete appreciation of the usual. This gift is not rare in the annals of English fiction; it would naturally be found in a walk of literature in which the feminine mind has laboured so fruitfully. Women are delicate and patient observers; they hold their noses close, as it were, to the texture of life. They feel and perceive the real with a kind of personal tact, and their observations are recorded in a thousand delightful volumes.[6]

This new sensibility, attitude, and social force was as revolutionary as the new genre that owed so much to it, and we would find similar cases in other countries. Even in Spain, land of the much touted and over-estimated "machismo," we find among the earliest and finest novelists the names of Cecilia Böhl von Faber and Emilia Pardo Bazán.

The early novelist thus advanced a new, revolutionary perspective from which to view life, replacing heroic action with sensitivity, national and societal standards with personal ones. Many novelists, in an effort to make their works as believable as possible, fell upon the letter form and the diary as logical methods of conveying the most personal concerns of characters. While the letter is as old as literature itself, the new epistles were not didactic, but deeply personal, and a natural vehicle for the process of individuation. The literary shift to the letter reflects the shift from an objective, external world view, to a subjective, individualistic one (Watt, p. 176). The novelist's private concerns are expressed through the portrayal of characters with whom artist and reader alike sympathize, and with whom they stand against the opposing world. All characters, moreover, are extensions of their creators; they incarnate the passions, the convictions, and the doubts of the author, and even the most insignificant ones are drawn from personal experience, as Scholes and Kellogg argue (p. 192). In creating sympathetic characters, through whom we are to see and experience the world, the novelist insures that we shall share their, and therefore his or her perspective.

---

[6]Henry James, "Anthony Trollope," in *The Art of Fiction and Other Essays* (New York: Oxford University Press, 1948), p. 50.

This perspective is critical of the surrounding world, a world which tends to be specific rather than abstract, a characteristic traceable to Stendahl: "Insofar as the serious realism of modern times cannot represent man otherwise than as embedded in a total reality, political, social, and economic, which is concrete and constantly evolving--as is the case today in any novel or film--Stendahl is its founder."[7] Again, however, we must insist that there be a degree of balance between character, world, and the conflict between them, or the genre is seriously threatened. One of the major and often irresistible temptations facing the novelist, particularly in provincial literatures, has been to succumb to the world he or she describes. Realism in countries with a strong individualistic impulse pays a great deal of attention to character and conflict and the critical perspective is normally maintained. Imported realism, however, too often becomes regionalism, resulting in interesting portraits of local color that fail artistically in international waters.

Such generally was the history of Spanish American fiction before the "Boom." Narrow regionalism, in which authors described meticulously a specific reality, has, according to José Donoso, been primarily responsible for the mediocrity of Spanish American fiction.[8] Donoso points out that such literature has been evaluated purely on the basis of the validity of its local color, not on literary merit. Thus the nations of Spanish America were not only isolated from the world, but from each other. The change of emphasis on the part of critics to literary quality is so recent that most of the authors responsible are still living, and many are relatively young.

That individuations should appear and thrive almost simultaneously in a number of Spanish American countries indicates that there is a high correlation between the success of the genre and a certain degree of cultural progress, of social preparedness. A brief examination of the history of the form in Europe confirms that certain minimal conditions must be met for it to thrive. While an in-depth look must wait until the next chapter, is is highly significant in understanding the role of the individuator as a social dissident that social

----

[7]Erich Auerbach, *Mimesis: The Representation of Reality in Western Literature*, trans. Willard R. Trask (Princeton: Princeton University Press, 1968), p. 463.

[8]José Donoso, *The Boom in Spanish American Literature: A Personal History* (New York: Columbia University Press, 1977), p. 15.

conditions in England in the latter part of the first half of the nineteenth century, for example, were in many ways similar to conditions in Spanish America in the fifth and sixth decades of the twentieth, and that England, under those conditions, experienced a boom of the novel quite like that of Spanish America over a century later.

Raymond Williams points out a rather startling and significant fact concerning the English novel: *Dombey and Son, Wuthering Heights, Vanity Fair, Jane Eyre, Mary Barton, Tancred, Town and Country*, and *The Tenant of Wildfell Hall* were all published within a period of twenty months. These years, 1847 and 1848, ushered in the great age of the Victorian novel, the stage for which had been set by several years of radical social changes:

> The changes in society had been long in the making: the Industrial Revolution, the struggle for democracy, the growth of cities and towns. But these also, in the 1840s, reached a point of consciousness which was in its turn decisive. The twelve years from Dickens' first novel to his radically innovating *Dombey and Son* were also the years of the crisis of Chartism. The first industrial civilisation in the history of the world had come to a critical and defining stage. By the end of the 1840s the English were the first predominantly urban people in the long history of human societies.[9]

With these changes in English culture came a new awareness, not only of an entirely new culture, but of a unified, new generation that arose with that culture and had to learn to survive in it. The novelists took it upon themselves to define and explore that generation, the culture in which it existed, and methods for survival. The boom in Spanish American fiction also coincides with sweeping cultural changes; including an industrial revolution, vast urbanization, and revolutions in Mexico and Cuba that led the Spanish Americans out of a stage of psychological colonialism to a sense of equality and independence. The French novel too followed close on the heels of a great social upheaval in which the individual was liberated and defined in new terms.

----

[9] Raymond Williams, *The English Novel from Dickens to Lawrence*, (New York: Oxford University Press, 1970), p. 9.

It would seem that the novel, at least individuation, always arises under similar circumstances: dramatic social change; the presence of strong political and social institutions; the emergence of a concept of the rights of each individual; a degree of tolerance of criticism. These basic ingredients are to be found in different areas of the world at different times, but Hauser's description of the European novel fits the genre no matter where or when it begins to flourish:

> The novel becomes the leading literary genre of the eighteenth century, because it gives the most comprehensive and profound expression to the cultural problems of the age--the antithesis between individualism and society. In no other form do the antagonisms of bourgeois society make themselves felt so intensely, in none are the struggles and defeats of the individual described so thrillingly. (*Social History*, pp. 737-738)

The "cultural problem" appears in Spanish America with force only in the twentieth century, but in Brazil was present decades earlier because of a radically different set of circumstances. World culture is not synchronous, and in each culture, often even in each country:

> The rise of the novel is associated with a new discovery of the isolation and autonomy of the private mind, with a sense of the absence of any preestablished harmony between the mind and what is outside the mind, with a diminishing faith in the existence of any supernatural power giving order and meaning to this world, and with a turning to relations between persons as the chief, if not exclusive, source of authentic life for the individual.[10]

The essential structure is clearly dialectical; it floats on the constant give and take that characterizes the interaction between the individual and a world in which these conditions have been met.

----

[10] J. Hillis Miller, "Three Problems of Fictional Form: First-Person Narration in *David Copperfield* and *Huckleberry Finn*," in *Experience in the Novel: Selected Papers from the English Institute*, ed. Roy Harvey Pearce (New York: Columbia University Press, 1968), p. 22.

To understand the role of the individuator as a social and cultural dissident we have to return to the heart of the artistic form: conflict and its nature. Different critics describe it in widely varying terms, but the essence is always the same. Lukács speaks of abstract and concrete potentialities and the individual's struggle to achieve them,[11] while René Girard maintains that all novels have a triangular pattern of desire: subject desires object because of a mediator. Girard argues that the protagonists of novels value the wealth, social prestige, mates, or whatever, of others, but even if the individual achieves these goals they do not bring happiness, for the character is isolated.[12] In essence, Girard, Lukács, and many others are all viewing novelistic conflict as the struggle of the individual for self betterment although they are interpreting it in different terms. Whether we prefer one of these interpretations, Hegel's view of the novel as the representation of the conflict between the poetry of the heart and the prose of antagonistic external conditions,[13] or Mark Schorer's "intersection of the stream of social history and the stream of the soul,"[14] or any of a number of other "definitions," we are concerned with the same substantial dialectic.

Contemporary writers often maintain this view, and more often than not their sympathies continue to lie with the individual in the struggle. Jerzy Kosinski's position is clearly that of an individuator:

> I guess I'm preoccupied in my nonfiction and in my novels with--what interests me most--the relationship between the individual and the group. During the war, as a child I lived in small villages, and as an outsider I couldn't help noticing

---

[11] Georgy Lukács, "The Ideology of Modernism," in *The Meaning of Contemporary Realism*, trans. John and Necke Mander (London: Merlin Press, 1963), pp. 22-23.

[12] René Girard, *Deceit, Desire, and the Novel: Self and Other in Literary Structure*, trans. Yvonne Freccero (Baltimore: The John Hopkins Press, 1965).

[13] G.W.F. Hegel, as interpreted by Alan Swingewood in *The Novel and Revolution* (Great Britain: Barnes & Noble, 1975), p. 7. Swingewood refers to Hegel, *Lectures on Fine Arts* (London: 1920), IV, pp. 26-73, 123-71.

[14] Mark Schorer, Forward to *Self and Society and Self in the Novel, English Institute Essays, 1955*, ed. Mark Schorer (New York, 1956), p. ix. Quoted by Alan Friedman in *The Turn of the Novel: The Transition to Modern Fiction* (London, Oxford, New York: Oxford University Press, 1966), p. 9.

how each peasant personified the whole village, with all its systems of beliefs, with all its systems of property. Perhaps then I realized that each of us is a microcosm of societal forces which operate outside and inside of us. I became aware of it again during the Stalinization of Poland, when for various political and ethnic reasons I was cast aside. By then, to a degree, I probably provoked some of it; I really didn't mind it. When I look at the pattern of my life I note that I often invite the penetrating force of society to approach me--and to reproach me--for not giving in, to remind me, as it were, where I stand as an individual. I considered ideology to be basically a form of fiction.[15]

This constant awareness of existence as an individual, and this reluctance to yield wholly to the group, is characteristic of all individuations. It is primarily responsible for the difficulties of Solzhenitsyn in Russia: "An individual's life is not always the same as society's. The collective does not always assist the individual. Each person has an abundance of problems which the collective cannot resolve. A person is a physiological and spiritual being before he becomes a member of his society. A writer's duty to the individual is no less than to society."[16]

The dissidence of individuations is not, as a rule, revolutionary, particularly if we interpret revolutionary as a positive concept, the establishment of a new political or social order. Such works may, at times, be revolutionary in a negative sense in that they seem to demand the destruction or at least the modification of some aspects of the old order, but once again prose fiction that argues *for* a structure, *for* a system of institutions and values, has a greater affinity with epic literature than with individuation. Within this general negativity, however, the degree of discontent may range broadly. Arnold Bennett held that: "The chief mark of the serious novelist, after fundamental creative power, is that he has a definite critical attitude

---

[15] Jerzy Kosinski, in an interview with Jerome Klinkowitz in *The New Fiction: Interviews with Innovative American Writers*, ed. Joe David Bellamy (Chicago: University of Illinois Press, 1974), pp. 164-65.
[16] Alexander Solzhenitsyn, in David Burg and George Feiffer, *Solzhenitsyn* (New York: Stein and Day/ *Publishers*, 1972), p. 240.

towards life,"[17] and Carlos Fuentes maintains that: "to create a text on nature or on social life is almost always a manner of denouncing the rigidity of both and of demanding change."[18] A problem encountered by many writers, and one that adversely affects a great number of novels, is the desire on the part of the novelist to advance a particular set of ideas rather than provide a more comprehensive vision of the individual interacting and conflicting with the social milieu. The conflict and the demand for change, the protest, the "everlasting no," are absolutely essential to individuations.

This type of novel is that form which has been located in the center of the mainstream of extended prose fiction for nearly two centuries. Its presence, indeed its dominance has been observed by many critics, but the term has required an adjective to assure that critic and reader are on the same path. Most have fallen back on "realistic," but others, trying to make the point clear, have hit upon different terms. Thus Everett Knight writes of the "classical novel," which he discerns as "that written between the end of the picaresque and the inauguration by Kafka of the contemporary novel."[19] "Classical novel" identifies that literary form that is here called individuation. That there is a distinct form apart from extended prose fiction and that this form is in fact that which is most faithful to the original and once prevailing concept of the novel is highlighted by René Girard's choice of terms, the "novelistic novel" (*Deceit*, p. 52). The complexity of the "novelistic novel," the "classical novel," the "realistic novel," or the individuation is due to the fact that the conflict is what sustains the structure. The individuator is in many ways supportive of both sides of opposition, and as the characters and situations change, so too changes the course of action. The possibilities within the genre are nearly infinite; the rise and fall of the genre is due more to external factors than to literary exhaustion.

----

[17]Arnold Bennett, "The Progress of the Novel," *The Realist*, 1 (April 1929), pp. 3-11. Quoted by Samuel Hynes, "The Whole Contention Between Mr. Bennett and Mrs. Woolf," *Novel: A Forum on Fiction*, 1.1 (Fall 1967), 42.

[18]"Dar un testimonio, fabricar un documento sobre la naturaleza o la vida social es casi siempre una manera de denunciar la rigidez de ambas y de exigir un cambio," Carlos Fuentes, *La nueva novela hispanoamericana* (México: Cuadernos de Joaquín Mortiz, 1969), p. 14.

[19]Everett Knight, *A Theory of the Classical Novel* (New York: Barnes & Noble, Inc., 1970), p. 4, note 3.

As Knight points out, the novelist criticizes society implicitly by creating identity for his characters and explicitly by revealing societal evils. *But*, he is also a defender of that society because his characters, as individuals, reinforce the societal values of the reader. Knight thus argues that Dickens was not a rebel, but a reformer, one who wished to preserve the major social structures but also to improve upon them. He believes, rightly perhaps, that the insistence on individualism in Western society (i.e. under capitalism) will be the death of that society. As we have seen, however, we now seem to be in retreat from extreme individualism. Its disappearance, moreover, will signal the death of individuation.

While it is essential to remember that individuation is a dissident art form, it is also crucial to keep in mind that it is not a tirade. Its content, its conflicts, are extremely complex, as is the relationship between the genre, the society that produces it and is in turn rendered within its pages, and the artist that serves as mediator. As Swingewood argues, the novel is liberal in its approbation of the individual, but conservative in its enshrinement of social values, for it reflects the bourgeoisie, "a class whose practices deny the values its ideology originally enshrined" (*Novel and Revolution*, pp. 33-34). This liberal/conservative dialectic suggests the complexity of the relationship between the novel and society, a complexity we must appreciate if we are to appreciate fully the value of individuation in both a social and an artistic sense. In short, the bourgeoisie, despite its individualistic orientation, is a class, and as such is inherently opposed to the threat of individualism, the very value upon which the class is founded. Thus the novelist, the individuator, "is opposed to a society and a social group that necessarily deny in practice the values that they implicitly affirm. Moreover, the novel with a problematic hero is, by its very structure, critical and realistic" (Goldmann. pp. 167-168). In all its aspects, the relation between artist, work, and society is highly dialectical and complex.

Even though the novel is identified with the bourgeoisie, it becomes most powerful and popular as an art form when the boundaries of that class have been clearly drawn, i.e. when the proletariat emerges as a threat. Individuation is thus liberal in that it criticizes bourgeois society, but conservative in that it defends its values: "The result is a highly complex dialectic between the form and content of the realist novel and bourgeois values. [Bourgeois realism represented] a revolutionary *and* a conservative art-form ... resonating yet criticising the values of modern capitalist culture" (Swingewood, p. 45). Moreover, just as individuation departs from literary tradition in that it criticizes while at the same time defending society, it also criticizes while it defends the individual. Thus it is more often than not ambiguous, as we might expect from such a highly mimetic art form. The presence of the ambiguous novel is a significant key to the appearance and trajectory of the genre in any given cultural context, for it signals the change from a prose fiction that espouses external values based on good and evil, patriotic and treasonous, moral and immoral, etc., to one that seeks to understand, fully portray, and defend the complexities of the individual in interaction with society. What Carlos Fuentes sees as a major change in the Spanish American novel, the appearance of ambiguous heroes in the novels of the Mexican Revolution, is in reality far more important than a mere modification of the novel (*Nueva novela*, p. 15). Works such as *Los de abajo* (1915) signal the beginnings of individuation in Spanish America.

The novel need not abandon its ambiguity, which stems from the attempt to present an honest, authentic account of the life of an individual or individuals in society, to indict those aspects of a character or social milieu that the author finds particularly blameworthy. Some authors, and some characters, are naturally more openly hostile than others. Stendahl's *The Red and the Black* is highly significant because the lines of conflict are so sharply drawn: "Julien Sorel is the first hero in a novel to be constantly aware of his plebeian birth, and to regard every success as a victory over the ruling class and every defeat as a humiliation" (Hauser, p. 743). Because of the carefully mimetic portrayal and its resulting ambiguity, polemics arise over the "true meaning" of works and over the "intentions" of creators. Thus in the twentieth century Jane Austen was re-evaluated and discovered to be not a meek, gentle depicter of social intercourse, but a fierce dissident by D.W. Harding.[20]

Despite the possibility of disagreement over a novelist's meaning and intention, it is clear that mimetic representation of the key ingredients of individuation--character, social setting, conflict--will lead to

----

[20] D.W. Harding, "Regulated Hatred: An Aspect of the Art of Jane Austen," *Scrutiny*, 8 (1940), cited by David Lodge, "Crosscurrents in Modern English Criticism," in *The Novelist at the Crossroads and Other Essays on Fiction and Criticism* (Ithaca: Cornell University Press, 1971), p. 270.

dissidence in one form or another, although in varying degrees. In Spanish America, which is certainly the epicenter of the contemporary novel, authors are particularly vocal in calling attention to the novelist as rebel:

> To write novels is an act of rebellion against reality, against God, against the creation of God, which is reality. It is an attempt to correct, change, or abolish true reality and substitute the fictitious reality that the novelist creates. The novelist is a dissident: he creates an illusory life, he creates verbal worlds because he does not accept life and the world as they are (or as he believes them to be). The root of his vocation is a feeling of dissatisfaction with life: each novel is a secret deicide, a symbolic murder of reality.[21]

Mario Vargas Llosa, the author of this quote, speaks with considerable authority, not only as a major twentieth-century novelist, but as an important literary critic, and John Hawkes makes an almost identical claim:

> It seems to me that fiction should achieve revenge for all the indignities of our childhood; it should be an act of rebellion against all the constraints of the conventional pedestrian mentality around us. Surely it should destroy conventional morality. I suppose all this is to say that to me the act of writing is criminal. If the act of the revolutionary is one of supreme idealism, it's also criminal. Obviously I think that the so-called criminal act is essential to our survival.[22]

---

[21]"Escribir novelas es un acto de rebelión contra la realidad, contra Dios, contra la creación de Dios que es la realidad. Es una tentativa de corrección, cambio o abolición de la realidad real, de su sustitución por la realidad ficticia que el novelista crea. Este es un disidente: crea vida ilusoria, crea mundos verbales porque no acepta la vida y el mundo tal como son (o como cree que son). La raíz de su vocación es un sentimiento de insatisfacción contra la vida; cada novela es un deicidio secreto, un asesinato simbólico de la realidad." Mario Vargas Llosa, *García Márquez: Historia de un deicidio* (Barcelona: Barral Editores, S.A., 1971), p. 85.

[22]John Hawkes in an interview with Robert Scholes in *The New Fiction*, ed. Joe David Bellamy, p. 108.

The criminal nature of writing is precisely why individuation can appear only in societies that are tolerant of social dissidence, and why it must disappear or at least go underground or into exile when the society becomes intolerant.

The antipathetic relationship between character and society is a reflection of the antagonism the writer feels. There is an infinity of possible sources, but the important fact is that the writer is out of step with the world:

> The causes of this rebellion, the origen of the vocation of the novelist, are multiple, but all can be defined as a warped relationship with the world. Because his parents were too indulging or too severe with him, because he discovered sex very early or very late or because he did not discover it at all, because reality treated him too well or too badly, because of weakness or strength, generosity or egotism, this man, this woman, in a given moment found themselves unable to accept life as their time, their society, their class or their family understood it, and they discovered their discrepancy with the world.[23]

Even though Nathalie Sarraute maintains that traditional "believable" and "live" characters are gone,[24] the very novelists she discusses (Faulkner is an example) offer us a vision, seen from the inside perhaps, but for all that, a vision of a personality, a perspective, a cohesive point of view, and this perspective, like the fully visible, fully delineated character of yore is in conflict, in collision with the forces

----

[23] "Las causas de esta rebelión, origen de la vocación del novelista, son múltiples, pero todas pueden definirse como una relación viciada con el mundo. Porque sus padres fueron demasiado complacientes o severos con él, porque descubrió el sexo muy temprano o muy tarde o porque no lo descubrió, porque la realidad lo trató demasiado bien o demasiado mal, por exceso de debilidad o de fuerza, de generosidad o de egoísmo, este hombre, esta mujer, en un momento dado se encontraron incapacitados para admitir la vida tal como la entendían su tiempo, su sociedad, su clase o su familia, y se descubrieron en discrepancia con el mundo." Vargas Llosa, *Historia de un deicidio*, p. 85.

[24] Nathalie Sarraute, "The Age of Suspicion," in *Approaches to the Novel: Materials for a Poetics*, ed. Robert Scholes, rev. ed. (San Francisco: Chandler Publishing Co., 1966), pp. 207-217.

operant around it. In fact contemporary dissidence is frequently more extreme than that of the traditional novel. And, as in the traditional novel, the center of consciousness is within the work, not outside as so often is the case in social novels in which characters and action are carefully controlled. Complexity is clearly not incoherence, and today, as always, writers write about themselves and their experiences.

John Barthes comes very near to declaring fiction man's primary defense against science. Instead of seeing characters as ourselves, we find assurance in seeing ourselves as characters:

> You and I still imagine ourselves to be characters, and our lives are influenced by other people around us whom we see as characters and our relations to whom we perceive in a dramatic, in a dramatical, way. As individuals we still live in calendar and clock time; no matter how that time may be discredited by physicists, it's nevertheless the kind of time we live in during most of our waking experience. "Microscopes and telescopes," Goethe says simply, "distort the natural focus of our eyes." The metaphysics of cause and effect, for example, may be extremely debatable. But the fact is that we live our lives most of the time with a very simple, crude, and perhaps old-fashioned understanding of cause and effect. We *have to*.[25]

Individuations may thus be our vital link with that which we like to believe is reality. Our lives, like our fiction, may require a willing suspension of disbelief. Moreover, individuations provide us a defense against our world, giving form and voice to our own discontent. The form "is essentially critical and oppositional. It is a form of resistance to developing bourgeois society."[26] The positive hero, once the central figure of the epic and later of socialist realism, is far more epic than novelistic, and has a very difficult time finding a place in individuation, particularly as protagonist.

----

[25]John Barthes in an interview with Joe David Bellamy in *The New Fiction*, ed. Joe David Bellamy, pp. 15-16.
[26]Lucien Goldmann, *Towards a Sociology of the Novel*, trans. Alan Sheridan (London: Tavistock Publications Limited, 1975), p. 13.

The novelist who advances positive views has a somewhat better chance than the positive hero, perhaps, but there are very few such writers of high quality, if indeed there are any. Lukács' reading of Tolstoy as a man who sought to convert readers to his point of view is baffling: "Tolstoy never practised art for art's sake. For him art was always the communication of certain contents and the artistic form the means of winning over his readers to his views."[27] If Tolstoy was indeed dedicated to converting his readers it was to convert them to his negative, reactionary, iconoclastic views. He does not preach sermons *for* certain values, but exposes, through examples, how petty, false, stupid, and inhumane were many of the values held by the society of his time. Tolstoy himself, in a quote cited earlier, seems to have anticipated and refuted in advance Lukács' claim: "If I were to be told that I could write a novel whereby I might irrefutably establish what seemed to me the correct point of view on all social problems, I would not even devote two hours' work to such a novel."[28]

The individuator's perspective on society, on values, on life, is negative and oppositional. As Graham Greene once remarked, "Isn't disloyalty as much a writer's virtue as loyalty is the soldier's? For the writer . . . is the defender of the individual."[29] Greene readily admitted that loyalty to his craft made him disloyal to the Catholic Church, and his most significant work, *The Power and the Glory*, was condemned by the Vatican.[30] The first novel encountered the same resistance some three hundred years earlier. In fact, *Don Quixote* was systematically banned in the colonies. A great number of individuations have merited the official ban, just as many have been politically censored, both of which are actions that can often be anticipated since the form steps forward to defend the individual and oppose institutions. Vargas Llosa's novelist as deicide is not unique;

----

[27]Georgy Lukács, *Studies in European Realism: A Sociological Survey of the Writings of Balzac, Stendhal, Zola, Tolstoy, Gorki, and Others*, trans. Edith Bone (London: Hillway Publishing Co., 1950), pp. 194-195.

[28]Leo Tolstoy, Letter to Peter D. Boborykin, 1865, in *War and Peace*, trans. Louise and Aylmer Maude, ed. George Gibian, Norton Critical Edition (New York: W.W. Norton & Company, Inc., 1966), p. 1360.

[29]Graham Greene, quoted by Eduardo Mallea in *Poderío de la novela* (Buenos Aires: Aguilar, 1965), p. 97.

[30]See David Lodge, "Graham Greene," in *The Novelist at the Crossroads*, p. 89.

it echoes in the works of Graham Greene and even Dostoevski. As Alyosha says in *The Brothers Karamazov*, "I am not rebelling against my God. I simply don't accept His world."[31] The refusal to "accept His world" may manifest itself in a wide variety of ways. Don Quixote seeks to recapture an idealized (unjustifiably) past, and disillusionment became a major theme for the novel:

> This new type of novel [Balzac's *Lost Illusions*] was the novel of disillusionment, which shows how the conception of life of those living in a *bourgeois* society--a conception which, although false, is yet necessarily what it is--is shattered by the brute forces of capitalism . . . . The first great novel, Cervantes' *Don Quixote* is also the story of lost illusions. But in *Don Quixote* it is the nascent *bourgeois* world which destroys the still lingering feudal illusions . . . . (Lukács, *European Realism*, p. 47)

It is not, of course, only the bourgeois world or capitalism that is capable of shattering illusions.

The struggle of the individual to survive, more often psychologically than biologically, typifies individuation throughout its history, although the nature of the struggle varies widely. Romanticism, naturally, produced protagonists that were more heroic than those of subsequent periods. Auerbach sees Stendahl himself as something of a romantic hero. In fact his description of the French novelist sounds more than a little like a description of Don Quixote:

> Such traits make him appear a man born too late who tries in vain to realize the form of life of a past period; other elements of his character, the merciless objectivity of his realistic power, his courageous assertion of his personality against the triviality of the rising *juste milieu*, and much more, show him as the forerunner of certain later intellectual modes and forms of life . . . . the stylistic level of his great realistic novels is much closer to the old great and heroic concept of tragedy than is that of most later realists--Julien Sorel is much more a "hero" than the characters of Balzac, to say nothing

---

[31] Fyodor Dostoewski, *The Brothers Karamazov*, Part III, Ch. 2, ed. Manuel Komroff (New York: Signet Books, 1958), p. 314.

of Flaubert. (*Mimesis*, pp. 465-466)

Sorel is indeed more heroic than many, or even most, later novel heroes.

The decline of heroic stature has been steady, as Northrop Frye has argued,[32] but is also a natural progression as the perspective of the individuator gradually replaced that of the epic poet and the romancer. Lukács' analysis of the increasing negativity of characters leads to the conclusion that novelistic protagonists eventually came to embody a "pure absence of ideas" and, for Lukács, inferior works, even in the case of Dickens.[33] Here, once again, it would seem that Lukács' social perspective has led him to misread badly. It is most difficult to imagine a reading of either *Bleak House* or *Great Expectations* that could ignore the conflicts in those works, or one that could discern a victory for social institutions or mores. If the novel had become what Lukács suggests, we would have had a mere continuation of the epic tradition, with the individual eagerly towing the line and doing whatever society might prescribe. Lukács' preoccupation with "typical" characters and his contempt for "modernism" are also by-products of his socialist mental set. As Swingewood argues, some of the great characters from authors Lukács most admired are not "typical":

> ... these egoistic individuals are eccentrics whose values place them in conflict with their society.... The inner life of the problematic hero, the revolutionary aspect of bourgeois realism which affirms the autonomy of the individual, is precisely what is meant by modernism. (*Novel and Revolution*, pp. 56-57)

Lukács' arguments fail when the heroes of the novel evolve to the point that they no longer represent a reaction to capitalism and the bourgeoisie that coincides, or would seem to coincide with a proletarian perspective. His views are applicable to a rather limited portion of the novel's history.

---

[32]Northrop Frye, *Anatomy of Criticism: Four Essays* (New York: Atheneum, 1967), pp. 33-35.
[33]Georgy Lukács, *The Theory of the Novel*, trans. Anna Bostock (Cambridge, Mass.: The MIT Press, 1971), p. 107.

Modernism is a continuation of realism and of romanticism. The psychological novel, which is a most logical and natural form of individuation, continues the dialectical relation between the individual and his world, and is just as mimetic as were the realistic novels of the nineteenth century. As Leon Edel has shown, the subjective novel is in many ways a return to the sensibilities of romanticism, though not a rebirth of the romantic hero as such (*Psychological Novel*, pp. 140-141). The main axis of similarity that runs through such novels as *Ulysses*, *Remembrance of Things Past*, and hundreds of works from *Don Quixote* down to *The Real Life of Alejandro Mayta* (Vargas Llosa, 1984) is their capacity for individuation, the dissidence, the negativity of perspective that rightly or wrongly isolates the individual and brings him or her into conflict with the world.

While at the heart of individuation lies the struggle for personal freedom and self-determination, it would be a mistake to conclude that the form must endorse these values as abstract goals in a positive manner. Tolstoy, while adamantly refusing to advance social causes or attempt to correct social ills, on the other hand laboriously argues against the absolute freedom and power of the individual, and even against clearly definable causes of actions and events. For him, every significant social movement or action is the result of extremely complex forces, many of which may come into play as a result of historical coincidence. Tolstoy thus holds dear exactly those forces that make great individuations: oppositional struggling forces, ambiguities, confusion, and conflict.

The question whether to sacrifice the individual for the sake of society or preserve him or her to the detriment of that society is not easily resolved, and a final answer is seldom even attempted in an individuation. The passionate discussions between Naphta and Settembrini in "Of the City of God, and Deliverance by Evil," Chapter Six of Mann's *The Magic Mountain*, is a debate on precisely this issue, but a conclusion is never reached. Mann and most other novelists would seem to believe that a middle course is necessary. Similarly, many might be somewhat sympathetic toward the Church's position in the "Grand Inquisitor" episode of *The Brothers Karamazov*. Freedom may well be bought at the expense of happiness, and may bring more harm than good to those who possess it. However, if a writer were to accept that view and write against freedom, he would cease to write individuations.

It is evident that a dissident perspective is more important to individuation than is the element of fiction. Truman Capote does not condone murder in *In Cold Blood* but he summons up a great deal of reader sympathy for Perry Smith through making the character so well-known to us that we can understand his perspective. The novel does not generate any hostility toward the values of rural Kansas society, but we come to feel that Smith is a victim of a larger social problem just as clearly as the Clutters are victims.

Not all individuations are typified by social dissidence alone. The negativity of the form often leads to a strongly evident literary dissidence as well. Although few novels flaunt their rejection or disdain for tradition so openly as do *Don Quixote, Tristram Shandy, Ulysses*, or even *Tres tristes tigres* or *Niebla*,[34] each work tends to stand as a counterpoint to all others: "a true novel imitates critically, not conventionally; hence it becomes a parody of other novels, an exception to prove the rule that fiction is untrue."[35] A number of outstanding novelists, including Thackaray, Trollope, and Unamuno, insisted on the falsity of their stories, but in so doing, created a psychological sympathetic bond between reader and character that leads to an ultimate acceptance of their fictions as fact. Henry James believed such a ploy to be "suicidal" (*The Art of Fiction*, p. 59), but it was generally highly effective. Two post-Jamesian writers, Unamuno and Borges, would cement a bond between the story-teller and God, and readers came to recognize that their own lives were precisely like those of the characters in fiction: all are the helpless victims of external manipulation and caprice.

Nonetheless, even those characters that are most keenly aware of their own impotence struggle fiercely to the end, if for no other reason than to protest as loudly as possible the injustices of life. In such works the inherent negativity of the individuation is all the more poignant as characters lash out against their creators and by extension, human beings lash out against their gods. The key factor from a generic point of view is that these works are manifestations of dissatisfaction, of protest, of dissidence from social and religious values.

----

[34] Guillermo Cabrera Infante's *Three Trapped Tigers* (1965) and Miguel de Unamuno's *Mist* (1914).

[35] Harry Levin, *The Gates of Horn: A Study of Five French Realists* (New York: Oxford University Press, 1963), p. 51.

Dissidence, whether literary, social, or moral, if allowed to become excessively vehement, cannot produce individuations. It is not possible to establish clearly drawn boundaries, for many of the greatest examples of the genre exist on the fringes, and indeed owe their greatness, at least in part, to their success in enlarging without overstepping those boundaries. Conservative attempts, on the other hand, often result in inferior literary artefacts.

The scientific perspective of naturalism would seem to be a conservative approach to fiction in that since novels pretend to be real, and claim mimesis as a primary goal, scientific, objective observation must surely provide the most direct path to greatness. Unfortunately, a dry, scientific approach fails to engage the reader's sympathy for the characters except in an abstract way, and the purely naturalistic novel becomes propaganda rather than art, for its concern is not *an* individual and personal struggles, but the social whole. Thus "naturalism (as the nineteenth century understood it) was never anything more than a blind alley" for fiction.[36] The gravity and immediacy of the social problems exposed by the naturalistic school led to its fiction being taken far more seriously than could be the case for the more artistic individuations that concerned themselves with relatively insignificant, abstractly speaking, individuals and their comparatively petty day to day concerns. This is not to say that the story of an individual cannot or does not involve the greater problems of society, but that novelists and readers alike became obsessed with the larger picture much to the detriment of the more personal one.

The novel thus, after an auspicious start, became in some countries an instrument of propaganda, and grew increasingly provincial, isolated, and serious. This tendency is obvious not only in France, where Zola dominated, but in those countries that looked to France as the primary source of literary excellence and most eagerly imitated French artists. Thus the novelists of Spain, Portugal, Brazil and Spanish America were particularly susceptible to this new seriousness, and only the truly great artists were able to produce work of lasting aesthetic value. The formula was quite simple: imitate Zola, but use local settings, minutely described and painfully rendered, and dwell increasingly on the sordid, the ugly. The damage was particu-

----

[36]Martin Turnell, *The Novel in France* (New York: Vintage Books, 1958), p. x.

larly keen in Spanish America, where naturalism flowed neatly into social realism, and where the concepts of literary experimentation, aesthetics, and the value of the unique individual were retarded for decades:

> ... in addition to being unmistakable ours, as the *criollistas* wanted, the novel should be, above all else, "important," "serious," an instrument which would be directly useful to social progress. Any attitude which might be accused of leaving the bad taste of something that might be labelled "estheticism" was anathema. Formal experimentation was prohibited. The architecture of the novel and its language were to be simple, flat, colorless, sober, and poor. (Donoso, p. 16)

Not only does this attitude destroy fiction as art, but it denies entrance to the individual. Each story cannot be "novel" for there is no tolerance for difference. The fiction of naturalism and social realism is thus often collective, and as such belongs properly to the epic tradition. As Fielding points out in his preface to *Joseph Andrews*, surely if a work is epic in all but meter, it must still be a member of that genre.

More often than not, individuation as a literay form is simply an exploration. The novelist creates characters and situations and follows the course of their interactions. As society has grown increasingly complex, value structures have tended to fragment and make difficult not only epic literature but individuation as well, for characters seem to exist in a moral vacuum of isolation. Individuation depends heavily on conflict between personal desires and rigid societal structures; when the structures have collapsed, we are left with only a portion of the necessary ingredients. Until such collapse, however, individuation probes and exposes changing values, and, because what it seeks to explore is unstable, the novel form itself is unstable as well: "Uncertainty about form is usually a sign of crisis in the development of an artist; in the case of novelists the crisis is often in a shifting conception of society, a changing vision of the relations between individual minds and the collective mind."[37] Needless to say,

---

[37] Allen Trachtenberg, "The Journey Back: Myth and History in *Tender is the Night*," in *Experience in the Novel*, ed. Roy Harvey Pearce, p. 133.

as the collective mind fragments, the uncertainty of the novelist increases.

Nonetheless, novelists have felt an obligation to continue their explorations, even though the results of their efforts are not as satisfying as they often were under more stable conditions. Much of what Lukács finds repugnant in modernism is not at all the result of inferior artists, but of different and rapidly changing social conditions that led to "a search for values that no social group defends effectively . . ." (Goldmann, p. 10). The form that once exposed and questioned mores has thus come more and more to deal with situations that are not specifically supported by any value system at all. A major search for meaning has been conducted by those novelists who have sought in the human psyche an antidote for crumbling or meaningless societal structures, but the result has often been disenchantment even with the individual: "mimetic characterization, if pushed far enough, leads to its own destruction" (Scholes and Kellogg, p. 202). Indeed, the invocation of myth and archetypal patterns and heroes has been made necessary by the disintegration of meaningful structures in many societies.

We have thus come full circle in many societies to arrive once more in a world of mystery and chaos to which the artist must counterpose order and meaning. Much of the world again requires epic and romance to restore coherence and purpose, circumstances under which the individuator is hard pressed to survive. There are, however, countries and even continents in which individuations have been heretofore impossible for more specific reasons and where they have only recently begun to thrive. The remainder of this study is an exploration of the history and the future of the genre under widely varying political and social conditions, and demonstrates clearly the precarious existence, yet the continued good health of the form.

CHAPTER FIVE

A Cultural and Historical Overview

The recognition of dissidence as a *sine qua non* of individuation gives rise to many speculations concerning the history and future of the genre, and also suggests a number of seeming anomalies that merit close investigation. How, for instance, could the first example be produced in always Catholic and almost always conservative Spain? Why did the greatest flowering of Russian individuation occur during the time of the Czar? If, as Orwell affirms, "Good novels are not written by orthodoxy-sniffers, nor by people who are conscience-stricken about their own unorthodoxy. Good novels are written by people who are *not frightened*,"[1] then why do novels, including excellent individuations, appear in societies in which we would expect social critics to be somewhat frightened?

The answers to such questions are extremely complex, and vary greatly from situation to situation. A major component of any response is that the individuator is as a rule not out to condemn society, any more than he or she gives it unreserved endorsement: "The novelist, much more than the poet, *must* be endowed with 'negative capability'; as he surveys the crowded human scene he must much more be able to withhold final judgment, to suspend his attachment to a particular point of view, to reconcile disparities . . . ."[2] Since the novelist offers neither condemnation nor endorsement, he or she may not always seem a threat to the *status quo*, and even in a rigid society may be able to slip through the chinks. Indeed some of the more fascinating examples of individuation are masterpieces of just such evasion: "part of the distinctive quality of much literature may derive from the delightful or sombre evasions and obliquities of an author asserting his freedom in a closed society" (Harvey, p. 25). However, a society may be closed--illiberal, monolithic, or coercive-- without seeming to be so at the administrative level, and on the other hand, may be far more tolerant than its institutional structures sug-

---

[1] George Orwell, "Inside the Whale," in *A Collection of Essays by George Orwell* (New York: Harcourt Brace Jovanovich, Inc. 1953), pp. 241-242.

[2] William John Harvey, *Character and the Novel* (Ithaca, New York: Cornell University Press, 1965), p. 26.

gest. If these basic points are kept in mind, speculation about the seeming anomalies may turn up viable explanations, and cogent reasons for the rather spotty history of the form in many cultures begin to emerge.

Spain is generally considered to be the birthplace of the modern novel. With its rich tradition of epic, romance, and picaresque narratives, as well as its political, economic, and artistic grandeur in the fifteenth and sixteenth centuries, it seems logical that Spain should have led the world in a great number of artistic innovations, but not in the novel, which, as we have seen, has a history that is closely linked to the Industrial Revolution, a large bourgeoisie, and a rather liberal attitude toward political, social, and moral dissent. Cervantes was a soldier and then a prisoner of war, either of which would tend to arouse in him a great spirit of nationalism, the sort of spirit that should produce epic literature. When he returned to Spain, instead of being rewarded for his loyal service he was ignored until some seventeen years later when he was imprisoned for financial irregularities, factors that we might expect to produce biting satires and picaresque tales. When he published the first volume of *Don Quixote*, the fifty-eight year old Cervantes had led a largely vagabond life, and had been almost systematically excluded from those social circles to which he aspired, yet the extreme bitterness we might expect does not show through in his novel. That Spain should be the birthplace of the novel is due to her previous literary history, a most peculiar politico-sociological situation at that precise moment in history, and the genius of Cervantes.

The literary background has been amply studied and documented. Spain had one of the greatest traditions of pure romance: chivalric, pastoral, and sentimental novels, all vehicles for pure idealism. Furthermore, Spain had a literary tradition of strong realism, and had at the end of the fifteenth century produced a major link to the modern novel, *La Celestina*, by Fernando de Rojas, in which characters, particularly lower class characters, began to assume some importance as individuals. Then in the sixteenth century Spain produced another vital link, the first picaresque novel, *Lazarillo de Tormes*. Cervantes juxtaposed the idealistic world of romance to the ironic world of the picaresque. The interplay between the two not only gave him his structure, but also yielded the type of conflict that we have identified with individuation. Fantasy (idealism, desire, aspiration) in the person of Don Quixote, struggles against the harsh reality of Cervantes'

Spain. Don Quixote is not unique in his idealism; the innkeeper (Pt. I, Ch. 31) and numerous others encountered by the Knight of Sad Countenance prefer fantasy as well, and even Sancho Panza, the personification of the reality principle, urges his master to marry the fictitious princess of Micomicón (Pt. I, Ch. 30). The opposing force of reality is painted vividly with copious mundane details that contrast sharply with the heroic world of romance that *Don Quixote* parodies, giving a sense of reality that is almost as intense as that of the picaresque. Don Quixote and Sancho are also portrayed in great realistic detail, but they acquire far more depth than picaresque heroes, partially because they are always more in the foreground than are their antagonists, and partially because their thoughts and their statements are more significant than their actions.

These considerations explain, at least in part, why *Don Quixote* must be considered the first modern novel, but do not answer what are more interesting questions for our purposes: how did Cervantes manage to publish such a work, why did it become so popular, and why does this one individuation stand so alone for over two hundred years in Spanish literary history? Until the late fifteenth century, Spain was ravaged by military struggles, an unstable situation that is not likely to produce individuations, for the private life of the individual can hardly be of major interest in times of overwhelming national crises. In the late fifteenth and sixteenth centuries Spain was a world power, involved in a grandiose enterprise of New World conquest, Catholic messianism, and European domination. The Monarchy ruled supreme, and in 1478 the Inquisition became a national institution. Again, the climate was hardly favorable for dissent.

At the precise time of *Don Quixote*, however, everything was radically changed. The king (Phillip III) was weak and ineffective, the military had suffered a number of humiliating defeats that shattered national confidence, the economy was in a shambles, with the major cities depopulated and industry failing badly. Only Madrid experienced growth, because of the influx of beggars. Moreover, Spain was involved in several foreign hostilities that were unpopular with the people, and finally, the Church itself was torn by rivalling factions, particularly the Jesuits and the Dominicans. The sudden collapse of Spain from greatness to near ruin was more than ample cause for popular dissent, and the weakness of the Crown coupled with the struggle within the Church allowed such dissent to be aired publicly for a short period of time. While the Monarchy never regained the power of the past, by the end of the seventeenth century the Church came down hard on dissidents and began to prohibit heterodox publications. In the eighteenth century Spain was enmeshed in her lengthy struggle with France and so the ideal conditions for individuation--a sense of national identity, a degree of social and political stability, a sense of esteem for the individual, and tolerance of open dissent--were long in coming. Even if Spain had not lost her sense of national stability and identity, it is unlikely that the tradition of individuation would have survived, for no European country embraced neoclassicism with its insistence on order, on working for the moral and social good, more vehemently.

Cervantes, unfortunately for him and fortunately for literature, wrote during a period of great disillusionment and decadence, and "showed the conscience of a writer torn between the reality of the present and the rhetoric of the past."[3] His ability to combine the literary traditions of Spain in one work and the peculiar conditions that encouraged publication of the result allowed the first individuation to appear without the existence of many of the conditions that we associate with its rise.

There are a number of factors critical to a climate favoring the rise and dominance of individuation that while related to the rise of the bourgeoisie and technology are equally important in their own right, particularly when the genre is viewed in a world context. Primary among these is a sense of national consciousness and identity, of unified community. This is not the same as a unifying spirit of nationalism such as can be found in most nations during times of grave crises, such as war, and which will actually inhibit individuation. During a period of great national expansion and imperialism, particularly if the people of the expanding power support the expansion, there is apt to be great optimism and little dissent, so the genre will not prosper. On the other hand, nor will it thrive in the colonies, for there the inhabitants are either engaged in epic struggles against the frontier, or are fighting to liberate themselves from the yoke of imperialism. The fight for survival or for independence is too grandiose to permit concern for the ordinary day-to-day concerns of the relatively unimportant individual.

---

[3]Jaime Vicens Vives, *Approaches to the History of Spain*, trans. Joan Connelly Ullman (Berkeley and Los Angeles: University of California Press, 1967), p. 104.

This is why Latin Americanists' concern that the novel form is late in arriving for them is totally unjustified. It is true that individuation arrives far later than in Europe, but it is because of Spanish America's colonial status and the relatively recent acquisition of national identity by most Spanish American countries. If we compare Spanish America with the United States, we can readily see that individuation began to flourish there much earlier, relatively speaking, than in the North. Carlos Fuentes' overview would fit the literary histories of most former colonies: "the conquistador arrived in search of nature's treasures, not the personalities of men, and liberation, in the second decade of the nineteenth century, from the conquistador, also meant the conversion of alien nature into our nature."[4] In such isolation the social intercourse that typifies individuation is impossible. Characters, rather than being individuals, tend to be heroic if they have positive values, and demonic if they are negative. Transplanted Europeans, as Lukács points out, tend to be schematic and superficial because of their isolation.[5] In contrast to its history in Spanish America, the novel arrives and achieves excellence early in Brazil. This may well be due to the fact that Brazil acquired a sense of national identity and pride before Spanish America, for Brazil was unique in that the former colony actually became the seat of the Portuguese Empire in 1807 when the royal family fled from the invading French and established the throne in Rio de Janeiro. Moreover, in Brazil independence was quietly and peacefully declared in 1822 without the bitter strife and polarization of emotions that typified the revolutions in Spanish America and the United States.

Even long after independence the literature of the colonies of the New World has its own peculiar stamp because of the overwhelming presence of unconquered nature: "There is much more in America than *mores* ; in England, there is not much else."[6] Still another fea-

----

[4] " . . . el conquistador llegó en busca de los tesoros de la naturaleza, no de la personalidad de los hombres, y liberarse, en la segunda decada del siglo XIX, del conquistador, significaba también convertir la naturaleza enajenada en naturaleza propia." Carlos Fuentes, *La nueva novela hispanoamericana* (México: Cuadernos de Joaquín Mortiz, 1969), p. 11.

[5] Georgy Lukács, *The Historical Novel*, trans. Hannah and Stanley Mitchell (London: Merlin Press, 1962), p. 64.

[6] Paul West, *The Modern Novel* (London: Hutchinson University Library, 1965), p. 271.

ture of much New World fiction is, at least in the past, its Utopian spirit, a spirit that is antithetical to introspective, critical individuation. David Lodge's statement that American literature "is utopian in spirit, and saturated in the myths of paradise lost or regained, either celebrating the potentialities of the American Adam, or brooding over what went wrong,"[7] would apply equally well to the literatures of Spanish America, Brazil, and perhaps any "conquered" wilderness where man has had the opportunity to build anew. Individuation is much more likely to appear and thrive if it is written far from the frontier, in a much stabler society, and if it takes this relatively stable society as its subject, for here, far from the daily concerns for physical survival that characterize the frontier, the novelist can turn attention to the more intimate crises of individual characters in their daily social circumstances. As Frye observes, the novelist "needs the framework of a stable society."[8] Frontier literature tends to be epic simply because its required emphasis is on action, on physical survival and domination. In the novel "character is more important than action and plot, and probably the tragic or comic actions of the narrative will have the primary purpose of enhancing our knowledge of and feeling for an important character, a group of characters, or a way of life."[9]

Individuation is thus slow to develop in colonial situations, if indeed it develops at all. There are many countries in which it has yet to become a strong literary force, and many others in which it has only recently emerged:

> Modern Australian critics and novelists are concerned to show, as American critics were in the twenties, that their native literature has grown up. They feel that in the earlier rugged years their novels took on too much of the crudeness and materialism of the society that produced them. They lacked critical "insights" and the perspective that can

----

[7] David Lodge, "Utopia and Criticism: The Radical Longing for Paradise," in *The Novelist at the Crossroads and Other Essays on Fiction and Criticism* (Ithaca: Cornell University Press, 1971), p. 236.

[8] Northrop Frye, *Anatomy of Criticism: Four Essays* (New York: Atheneum, 1967), p. 305.

[9] Richard Chase, *The American Novel and its Tradition* (Garden City: Doubleday & Company, Inc., 1957), p. 12.

produce self-criticism without disloyalty .... This is not a "colonial" literature at all, but a newly self-conscious, self-efficient product, independent of its British ancestry.[10]

The achievement of a sense of identity, community, and equality is critical to the development of a strong tradition of individuation. Most non-European nations have been slow to reach such a state of awareness, and the twentieth century threatens to destroy it where it has been achieved. The lack of a sense of community and national consciousness can inhibit the development of individuation even in major countries, particularly those that are large and sparsely or unevenly populated. The brilliant though brief novelistic boom in Russia in the nineteenth century took place during what literary historian Marc Slonim calls a "blossoming of national consciousness"[11] and also corresponded to the right of private presses decreed by Catherine, which offered an opportunity for individuations to thrive.

National consciousness and a sense of community are not, however, sufficient. Nationalistic pride or arrogance are often intolerant of individual dissent and individuators are unable to find a press or an audience. A society must tolerate and encourage individualism and by extension criticism of its own structures and values. It is this trait that brought France and England to the fore and left Germany behind:

> The fact that Germany has had so few novelists of distinction is clarified by a remark of Andre Gide's: "The fatherlands of the novel are the lands of individualism." Admitting that German fiction lacks European significance, a sociological study has concluded that it identified itself too uncritically with the interests of the middle class. No land has been more self-critical or more individualistic than France, and no literature has spoken for all of Europe with more authority.[12]

---

[10]Susanne Howe, *Novels of Empire* (New York: Columbia University Press, 1949), p. 138.

[11]Marc Slonim, *The Epic of Russian Literature: From its Origens Through Tolstoy* (New York: Oxford University Press, 1950), p. 33.

[12]Harry Levin, *The Gates of Horn: A Study of Five French Realists* (New

The individuator does not speak for the nation or for the community or for the Church or even for the class; that is the role of epic: "What most makes the epic kind is a communal or choric quality. The epic writer must express the feelings of a large group of people living in or near his own time."[13]

Social groups can be as rigorous in surpressing individuation as authoritarian governments: "it is the social character's function *to mold and channel human energy within a given society for the purpose of the continued functioning of this society.*"[14] If German fiction has indeed "identified itself too uncritically with the interests of the middle class" it may simply be reflecting the effectiveness of such channeling. Coerced conformity, on the other hand, creates an urgent need for individuation, even though censorship may suppress it:

> In the conflict with the commands of one's conscience, in the fight against irrational authority, the personality developed--specifically the sense of self developed. I experience myself as "I" because I doubt, I protest, I rebel. Even if I submit and sense defeat, I experience myself as "I"--I, the defeated one. (Fromm, *Sane Society*, p. 153)

This smoldering sense of suppressed dissent under authoritarianism bursts to the surface when such governments are overthrown. During the rigid dictatorship of Fulgencio Batista in Cuba, for example, there were virtually no individuations published. The handful of Cuban individuations of that time were written and published in exile. Immediately after the fall of the dictator, many individuations that have gained international recognition for their excellence, novels by Alejo Carpentier, José Lezama Lima, Guillermo Cabrera Infante, Severo Sarduy and others, seemed to appear almost overnight. Then, as the Castro regime clamped down on dissenters, individuation vanished as suddenly as it had appeared.

York: Oxford University Press, 1963), p. 74.

[13] E.M.W. Tillyard, *The Epic Strain in the English Novel* (Fair Lawn, New Jersey: Essential Books, Inc., 1958), p. 15.

[14] Erich Fromm, *The Sane Society* (New York: Rinehart & Company, Inc., 1955), p. 79.

Italy provides an even more persuasive example of the importance of a sense of national identity and community combined with a tolerance of dissent. Italy's literary tradition is much older and nobler than those of France or England, yet her novel has been extremely sporadic and weak in comparison. Italian history has simply not been favorable to individuation. While Italy may not have been much worse off than the rest of Europe through the fifteenth century (although even this claim could be disputed), while other European nations were building, Italy continued to decline, and could hardly be properly called a country at all until the nineteenth century. In fact, from 1580 to 1814, "Italy was not a country, either geographically or sentimentally; it became instead a place of recreation for gentlemen on the Grand Tour."[15] The individual, constitutional government, and national independence were not championed before the Carbonari in the early nineteenth century. Eventually, after many years of foreign domination, factionalism, and turmoil, Italy was strongly unified and gained a sense of strength and national pride, but it became relatively stable only under Mussolini in the 1920's. As we might expect, individuation was non-existent under the fascist regime. Significantly, after World War II there has been a flurry of activity, much like that of Cuba in the first few years following the fall of Batista, but in Italy the boom has continued for there has been no censorship as there has been under Castro. Despite its literary greatness and dominance in the Middle Ages and Renaissance, then, Italy did not become a major force in the history of the individuation. Her novelistic tradition was relatively weak and sporadic all the way into the mid-twentieth century because of her political and cultural history. Individuation as a genre, indeed a single individuation as literary artefact, is far more than the product of a single writer's literary genius.

As the examples of nearly all nations under strong dictatorships show, individuation cannot thrive when the State controls the presses. The great period of the Russian novel coincides with the rather brief history of private and free press; the strength of the novelistic impulse in Spain, Italy, and Cuba is directly proportional to the amount of liberty accorded the press. State control of literature leads, perhaps without exception, to the use of literature as a didactic tool,

----

[15]Jack F. Bernard, *Up from Caesar: A Survey of the History of Italy from the Fall of the Roman Empire to the Collapse of Fascism* (Garden City, N.Y.: Doubleday & Company, Inc., 1970), pp. 298-299.

an instrument of education that argues for the preservation and the policies of the State, in short to a type of literature that is diametrically opposed to individuation. On the other hand, interludes between strongly centralized governments, such as that experienced in Cuba in the early 1960's, favor the form, as authors rush to express their long surpressed protestations of individual worth. In other cases, individuation has been forced into indefinite exile or has disappeared completely.

Centralization of publishing may come about under varying circumstances and for widely different reasons, however, and economic monopolies may pose as great a threat to individuation as a totalitarian dictatorship. We have earlier seen an example of this sort of economic censorship in Latin America, where, as José Donoso believes, insistence by the publishers on certain subjects and formulae severely retarded the development of a vital novelistic tradition. There the monopoly was finally broken by a foreign publisher, Carlos Barral of Spain, who took manuscripts from Spanish American authors to Spain, published them, and then exported them back to Spanish America. Barral was thus instrumental in the boom of Spanish American fiction in the 1960's.

In almost all cases, centrally controlled literature, particularly prose fiction, has been of poor quality. Whether we speak of the hundreds of examples of socialist realism emanating from the Soviet Union or Cuba, the rather innocuous regionalism of Chile, or the thousands of "drug-store" novels of the United States, the content is readily predictable in each case, and the aesthetic value is minimal. If there is such a thing as totalitarian literature (giving the noun its full aesthetic implication) it has yet to appear in any recognizable form:

> The atmosphere of orthodoxy is always damaging to prose, and above all it is completely ruinous to the novel, the most anarchical of all forms of literature. How many Roman Catholics have been good novelists? Even the handful one could name have been bad Catholics. The novel is practically a Protestant form of art; it is a product of the free mind, of the autonomous individual. (Orwell, p. 241)

The retreat from individualism as a positive value, the slow but steady centralization of the press in most countries, and the crumbling sense of community pose far more serious threats to literary individuation than does the exhaustion of subjects or themes.

The only strong antidote to the failing sense of community that has been proposed in the twentieth century, if we exclude the emotional and physical mobilizations that accompanied World War II, has been socialism. We have already touched upon some of the ways in which socialism works to the detriment of novelistic activity, but extended prose is the most characteristic form of literature in socialist countries, and therefore the socialist novel requires closer examination. If we wish to be precise in our terminology, we must admit that there is no such thing as a socialist individuation. There are a few that have socialist settings, socialist authors, or come from socialist countries, but the term "socialist novel" suggests a work that depicts and defends life under socialism, and individuation is incapable of advancing and defending social causes. The Utopian novel, which has a great deal in common with the socialist novel, is equally incapable of individuation.

Nevertheless, socialist governments, critics, and artists have a long-standing love affair with the novel form, for they see it, quite rightly, as the genre that depicted better than any other the evils of capitalistic society, and hence as one of the most powerful and significant forms of literature. At the heart of this love affair, however, lies a basic misunderstanding of the nature of the genre. Lukács did not see that negativity and the novel, at least in its most common form, go hand in hand, but believed the genre could limit its criticism to capitalist society: "It is thus that justified criticism of capitalist society degenerated into a despairing misrepresentation of objective reality itself."[16] He implies that had the newer realists but realized the virtues of socialism, they would have written optimistic novels. Socialists tend to agree that the novel should be pessimistic in depicting capitalism and optimistic in depicting socialism, but they are confusing two distinct genres, individuation and epic. The former values the individual above the social, the latter the social above the individual. Lukács discerns a "connection" between epic and novel without recognizing this opposition:

---

[16] Georgy Lukács, *Studies in European Realism: A Sociological Survey of the Writings of Balzac, Stendhal, Zola, Tolstoy, Gorki, and Others*, trans. Edith Bone (London: Hillway Publishing Co., 1950), p. 191.

> Within capitalist society the class struggle of the proletariat gives birth to aims which directly unite the individual and the social. These aims can never, of course be adequately realized in capitalist society, but epic literature can show their straight and unmistakable movement towards future fulfillment. (*Historical Novel*, p. 149)

For socialists, there is thus a dual role for narrrative, but particularly for the novel, and which role a work is to assume, individuation or socialization, is determined by the nature of the society in which it is written.

Once this theoretical perspective is accepted, critics need no longer concern themselves with the inner dynamics of literary genres, but can evaluate literature on its psychological and philosophical content *vis-a-vis* the society in which it was written. Thus Ernst Fischer recognizes two varieties of realism: critical realism and social realism. Good bourgeois art is critical, good socialist art is supportive:

> "Critical realism," and, more comprehensively, bourgeois literature and art in general (that is to say all great bourgeois art and literature) embodies a criticism of surrounding social reality. "Socialist realism," and, more comprehensively, socialist literature and art as a whole, embodies the fundamental harmony of the artist or writer with the goals of the ascending working class and socialist world.[17]

The possibility of a legitimate criticism of socialist reality or a legitimate positive portrayal of bourgeois society is unthinkable. According to this line of thought, individuation--the mainstream novel--is a legitimate form only under capitalism; epic is the logical and only legitimate art form under socialism.

---

[17]"El 'realismo crítico' y, más ampliamente, el arte y la literatura burgueses en general (es decir, todo el gran arte y la gran literatura burgueses) entrañan una crítica de la realidad social circundante. El 'realismo socialista' y, más ampliamente, el arte y la literatura socialistas en conjunto, entrañan el acuerdo fundamental del artista o escritor con los fines de la clase obrera y el mundo socialista ascendentes." Ernst Fischer, "El arte socialista," in Adolfo Sánchez Vázquez, *Estética y marxismo* (México: Ediciones Era, 1970), Vol. II, p. 319.

Nowhere is this fact more evident than in socialist thinking on the issues of individualism and freedom: "in the awareness that in contemporary bourgeois society individual freedom can only be corrupt and corrupting because it is a case of unilateral privilege based on the unfreedom of others, this desire [for freedom] must entail the renunciation of individual freedom."[18] Lukács goes on to argue that the key to the success of socialism is discipline, and in another essay defends the need for dictatorship in the early stages of revolution precisely because of the discipline it imposes: "Freedom cannot represent a value in itself.... *Freedom must serve the rule of the proletariat, not the other way around*" (*History and Class Consciousness*, p. 292). The concept of freedom, like that of individualism, has had to be redefined under socialism. Socialist thinkers are apparently able to define freedom and individualism only in negative terms. While they frequently allude to individual freedom under socialism, the nature of this freedom is extremely vague and mentioned only in passing, while the thrust of argumentation zeroes in on the evils of bourgeois freedom: "Above all one thing must be made clear: freedom here does *not* mean the freedom of the individual.... the "freedom" of the men who are alive is the freedom of the individual isolated by the fact of property which both reifies and is itself reified (*History and Class Consciousness*, p. 315). It should be obvious that if this is the line of thought of Lukács, the leading socialist authority on the novel, that individuation has no place in socialist society.

Lukács' arguments often become so confusing because while his is a brilliant literary mind, he loves both the novel as a genre and socialism as an ideology and he strives constantly to bring the two into harmony, an impossible task. Politicians are less apt to have their thoughts cluttered by aesthetic concerns:

> Will not Marxism-Leninism then destroy the creative spirit? Oh yes, it will. It will destroy the feudal, bourgeois, and petty-bourgeois creative spirit ... that is rooted in liberalism, individualism, abstractionism [and] that stands for art-

---

[18] Georgy Lukács, "Towards a Methodology of the Problem of Organization," in *History and Class Consciousness: Studies in Marxist Dialectics*, trans. Rodney Livingstone (Cambridge Mass.: The MIT Press, 1971), p. 315.

for-art's sake and is aristocratic, defeatist, and pessimistic.[19]

Raymond Williams, in his excellent study on Marxism and literature, points out that it is the deformation of the "social" into the "collective" and the additional tendency to impose on art through structuralism "an abstract model of determinate social structures and their 'carriers'" that has led many socialist sympathizers to retreat to the relative security of bourgeois society.[20] This has especially been the case for novelists.

Because of its lengthy history and its undeniable significance in interpreting and evaluating the culture from which it flows, art in all its forms is highly prized, and the control or suppression of artistic endeavors is likely to be most unpopular. All political systems seem to recognize this fact. Strong right-wing dictatorships, which do not rely on the support of the people, or at least that of the intelligentsia, do not concern themselves with popularity and hence make no apologies or explanations for the overt suppression and control of art. Socialist governments, on the other hand, either represent or pretend to represent the will and the best interests of the majority, and their relationships with the artistic community are somewhat more awkward and are accompanied by a sense of embarassment. Therefore, perhaps the most important word in all statements made by socialist leaders to artists and intellectuals is "but":

> We maintain that there should be democracy and liberty in the bosom of the people, *but* liberty should not be extended to counter-revolutionaries; we must exercise dictatorship over them . . . . It is necessary to establish a clear line between us and our enemies. (Lu Ting-Yi, 1956)[21]

* * *

----

[19]Mao Tse-Tung, *Problems of Art and Literature* (New York: International Publishers, 1950), pp. 44-45.

[20]Raymond Williams, *Marxism and Literature* (Oxford: Oxford University Press, 1977), p. 194.

[21]"Sostenemos que debe haber democracia y libertad en el seno del pueblo, pero que la libertad no debe extenderse a los contrarrevolucionarios; sobre ellos tenemos que ejercer la dictadura . . . . Es preciso establecer una clara linea entre nosotros y nuestros enemigos." Lu Ting-Yi, "Que cien flores se abran; que compi-

Each one is free to write and say everything he pleases without the slightest limitation. *But* every free association (including the party) is free to expel from its ranks anyone who, taking advantage of the name of the party, propagates points of view opposed to those of the party. (Lenin, 1905)[22]

* * *

Bearing in mind the general principles of the war of resistance and national unity, we must tolerate all works of literature and art expressing every kind and shade of political attitude. At the same time [*but*], we must be firm in principle and in our position . . . . This means we must criticize severely . . . works which present viewpoints that are opposed to national, scientific, mass, and Communist interests . . . . (Mao, *Art and Literature*, p. 37)

* * *

Within the revolution, everything. [*But*] Against the revolution, nothing. (Fidel Castro, 1961)[23]

* * *

It is harmful to the growth of art and science if administrative measures are used to impose one particular style of art and school of thought and to ban another. [*But*] as far as unmistakable counter-revolutionaries and wreckers of the

---

tan cien escuelas ideológicas," in Sánchez Vázquez, *Estética y marxismo*, Vol. II, p. 291. This quote is from a speech made by Ting-Yi, Head of the Department of Propaganda of the Central Committee of the Communist Party of China, in 1956.

[22]"Cada cual es libre de escribir y de decir todo aquello que le plazca sin la menor limitación. Pero toda asociación libre (inclusive el partido) es libre de expulsar de sus filas a todo aquel que, aprovechándose del nombre del partido, propaga puntos de vista antipartidistas." V.I. Lenin, "La organización del partido y la literatura del partido," in Sánchez Vázquez, *Estética y marxismo*, Vol. II, p. 370.

[23]"Dentro de la Revolución, todo; contra la Revolución, nada." Fidel Castro, "Palabras a los intelectuales," in *Fidel Castro* (Argentina: Cuadernos de la linea, n.d.), p. 10.

socialist cause are concerned, the matter is easy: we simply deprive them of their freedom of speech. (Mao, 1960)[24]

No one could be more counter-revolutionary or more deserving of expulsion or suppression than the artist who would defend the rights and needs of the individual as opposed to the mass or the nation, i.e., the individuator.

Aesthetics thus take on a marvellous simplicity under strong socialist regimes: if the leadership likes a work, i.e., if it supports the regime and suits its goals, the work is good; if not, then not only is it bad art, it is dangerous and must be suppressed:

> There are two standards for literary and art criticism. One is the political standard and the other the artistic standard. By the political standard, artistic production is good . . . if it serves the interests of our war of resistance and unity . . . . Conversely, artistic production is bad . . . if it encourages dissension and division among the masses . . . . (Mao, *Art and Literature*, p. 36)

* * *

> In any class society or in any class within that society, political standards come first and artistic standards second. (Mao, pp. 37-38)

* * *

> Whatever makes for the greater good of the majority of the people may be considered superior. (Mao, p. 31)

* * *

> If the Revolution has the right to destroy bridges and art monuments whenever necessary, it will stop still less from laying its hand on any tendency in art which, no matter how great its achievement in form, threatens to disintegrate the

---

[24]Mao Tse-Tung, quoted by Raymond Williams, *Marxism and Literature*, p. 203.

revolutionary environment or to arouse the internal forces of the Revolution, that is, the proletariat, the peasantry and the intelligentsia, to a hostile opposition to one another. Our standard is, clearly, political, imperative and intolerant. (Trotsky)[25]

* * *

We appraise cultural and artistic creations according to their utility for the people.... Our appraisal is political. There can be no aesthetic value without human content. There can be no aesthetic value opposed to justice, to the well-being, to the liberation, to the happiness of man. (Fidel Castro)[26]

* * *

Here things in general are clear. The fundamental criterion is the same as that of the proletarian ethic that has already been pointed out: that which contributes to the development and the victory of the proletarian cause is good, and that which impairs it is bad. (Anatoli Lunacharsky)[27]

These attitudes toward aesthetic questions, coming from the three major socialist powers, Russia, China, and Cuba, typify the socialist position. While they are clearly extremely damaging to aesthetics and artistic endeavors in general, they are absolutely devastating to the survival of literary individuation.

----

[25] Leon Trotsky, *Literature and Revolution*, trans. Rose Strumsky (Ann Arbor: University of Michigan Press, 1960), pp. 220-221.

[26] "Valoramos las creaciones culturales y artísticas en función de la utilidad para el pueblo.... Nuestra valoración es política. No puede haber valor estético sin contenido humano. No puede haber valor estético contra la justicia, contra el bienestar, contra la liberación, contra la felicidad del hombre." Fidel Castro, "El caso Padilla," in *Fidel Castro*, pp. 51-52.

[27] "Aquí las cosas en general están claras. El criterio fundamental es el mismo que el de la ética proletaria que ya se apunta: lo que contribuye al desarrollo y a la victoria de la causa proletaria es bueno, y lo que perjudica a ella es malo." Anatoli Lunacharsky, "Tareas de la crítica marxista," in Sánchez Vázquez, *Estética y marxismo*, Vol. I, p. 391. Lunacharsky was Russian Commissar of Education from 1917 to 1929.

Individuation is a vehicle for the artistic expression of dissent from the *status quo*, no matter who or what determines the composition or the nature of the latter. It is a maverick form that simply disappears before any attempt to make it conform and become a cog in the political machine, which is precisely what has happened under socialism: "We have called this meeting for the express purpose of making literature and art part of our revolutionary machinery, so that they may become a powerful weapon . . . " (Mao, *Art and Literature*, p. 8). This is not to say that socialist ideologists are opposed to literary individuation. To the contrary, they applaud it loudly, so long as it is a product of some capitalist society. It is only when it is written or takes place in socialist society that it becomes counter-revolutionary:

> Those who write subversive literature within the capitalist world, in the majority agree that once this order has been subverted and replaced by the revolutionary order, their subversive mission has been accomplished. To continue trying to subvert an order that would then be socialist would mean simply to wage a counter-revolution. It is an obvious rule: only the professional negators can fail to understand it.[28]

The problem for the serious individuator is quite obvious: he is by definition a "professional negator" and has no place in the revolutionary society.

Nonetheless, prose fiction is the most plentiful form of literature under socialism. It and theatre are most easily adapted for utilitarian educational purposes. Its language, form, and content can be made simple enough for mass consumption even by the nearly illiterate.

----

[28]"Quienes escriben literatura subversiva dentro del mundo capitalista, en su mayoría dan por sentado que, una vez subvertido ese orden y reemplazado por el revolucionario, su misión de subversión estará cumplida. Continuar tratando de subvertir un orden que entonces sería socialista, significaría sencillamente pasar a militar en la contrarrevolución. Es una regla de mínima coherencia: sólo los negadores profesionales pueden no entenderlo." Mario Benedetti, *El escritor latinoamericano y la revolución posible* (Buenos Aires: Editorial Alfa Argentina, 1974). pp. 74-75. Although an Uruguayan, Benedetti has for years been deeply involved in the Cuban revolution, and has served as official spokesman on artistic matters.

"Literature" becomes not only literature for the masses, but bulk literature of very low quality, as was the case in Russia under Stalin: "Conformist writers could flourish . . . supported by massive government subsidies and published not because of popular demand but simply through a slavish following of the correct political 'line.' Soviet literature quickly degenerated into a stifling mediocrity . . . ."[29] The novel alluded to here by Swingewood is clearly not individuation, but rather something more akin to the epic. The fate of the novel under Cuban socialism has been similar. There are only one or two works of extended prose fiction that maintain the party line but manage to salvage a degree of artistic merit. They are *La última mujer y el próximo combate* (The Last Woman and the Next Battle, 1971) by Manuel Cofiño López, and *Sacchario* (Sugar, 1970) by Miguel Cossío Woodward. Both have a good deal in common with the Soviet prose of the first Five Year Plan (1928-1933), and both meet the criteria for epic literature. The central theme of *Sacchario* is the need to sacrifice one's identity and individual rights for the good of the social whole. The protagonist of *La última mujer* is a genuine epic hero, Bruno, known as "Pedro the Bulldozer Operator," who sets a superb example for the Cuban worker and ultimately sacrifices his life for the revolution. Significantly, no Cuban work has won the prestigious national prize for the novel since 1971. Even Cubans seem to recognize that good novels come from other parts of the world (i.e. from capitalist societies).

For the most part socialist critics appear to be satisfied with this state of affairs. Lukács, however, who was endowed with a keen sense of aesthetic sensibility, was not favorably impressed, particularly with the literature of the Stalinist period:

> Literature ceased to reflect the dynamic contradictions of social life; it became the illustration of an abstract "truth": The aesthetic consequences of such an approach are all too evident . . . . the notion of literature-as-illustration was extremely detrimental to good writing.[30]

---

[29] Alan Swingewood, *The Novel and Revolution* (Great Britain: Barnes & Noble, 1975), p. 110.

[30] Georgy Lukács, "Critical Realism and Socialist Realism," in *The Meaning of Contemporary Realism*, trans. John and Necke Mander (London: Merlin Press,

Lukács was especially annoyed by "revolutionary romanticism":

> Thus, an otherwise interesting novel would be fatally marred by a scene in which a woman on a collective farm rejected the prize of a lamb she had herself brought up because communal is dearer to her heart than private property. Or a group of young Komsomols set out to win a harvest competition; they succeed in this by giving up their lunch-hour--only the strict orders of the superior can make them take some food and have proper rest. (*Contemporary Realism*, p. 129)

His anguish could only be increased if he were to read any of the dozens of similar examples produced in Cuba in the last twenty years.

Fortunately for the devotee of individuation, and perhaps unfortunately for the individuator, the latter is a hardy, even foolhardy breed, always trying to create and ever on the lookout for a chink in the political armor. Two noteworthy recent examples are Alexander Solzhenitsyn of Russia and Edmundo Desnoes of Cuba. Solzhenitsyn is the more famous, not only because he is Russian, but because of his political difficulties and subsequent exile. For all his international fame, he has hardly been published within Russia, where his books circulated in manuscript form until copies found their way to the West where they were published without the consent either of Russian authorities or of Solzhenitsyn himself. Only one novel was published in Russia, *A Day in the Life of Ivan Denisovich*, and it is not a sign that individuation can flourish in Soviet Russia, or even that it can survive. It was published in 1962, during the de-Stalinization program amid a relative flurry of novelistic activity. Even during this time *A Day in the Life* was considered sufficiently dangerous that it may not have been published at all were it not for the direct intervention of Khrushchev, who sought to prove that the days of repression were over.

Solzhenitsyn is not only a powerful writer, but a particularly dangerous one for the authorities. His realism is so acute that it is painful for the reader, and it is so factual that his depiction of life in a Soviet labor camp was certain to arouse the concern of the reading

---

1963), p. 119.

public. Perhaps no writer of the past thirty years has so vividly conveyed a sense of "real" life: "His realism is pre-eminently *factual* and thus specifically historical; there are few contrivances of plot or character . . ." (Swingewood, p. 251). Moreover, Solzhenitsyn is totally committed to the cause of the individual, to the problems of the individual that the collective cannot solve: "All forms of totalitarianism strike at the concept of the individual striving to eliminate every form of the conflict between the individual and society. Tragedy here flows from a refusal to submit to the requirements of such systems . . ." (Swingewood, p. 227). Solzhenitsyn's refusal to compromise in any way with Soviet authorities provoked an inevitable attitude and response, even in the Soviet Writers' Secretariat: "The works of Solzhenitsyn are more dangerous to us than those of Pasternak: Pasternak was a man divorced from life, while Solzhenitsyn, with his animated, militant, ideological temperament, is a man of principle."[31] Solzhenitsyn's fate was sealed by his own determination to be an individuator, a dissident voice.

Edmundo Desnoes and Alexander Solzhenitsyn have a good deal in common. Desnoes too is a powerful realist, his characters are isolated from and in conflict with the society that surrounds them, and he is unquestionably the author of the best, perhaps the only individuations produced from within and with the apparent blessing of the revolution.[32] Malabre, the protagonist of Desnoes' best novel, *Memories of Underdevelopment*, which was also made into the best film of the Cuban revolution, is, like the characters of Solzhenitsyn, totally alienated from the society that is actively involved in carrying out the revolution. Desnoes, however, was spared official wrath and censorship because all of his protagonists are what Cubans contemptuously call "gusanos" (worms). These are individuals who remained in Cuba after the revolution, in many cases living on income from reimbursements for confiscated businesses and property, or simply accepting subsistence checks. They work neither for nor against the revolution,

---

[31]Statement by Surkov during a session of the Soviet Writers' Secretariat, Sept. 22, 1967, convened to discuss the possible Russian publication of *Cancer Ward*. In Alexander Solzhenitsyn, *Cancer Ward*, trans. Nicholas Bethell and David Burg (New York: Farrar, Strauss and Giroux, 1969), p. 552.

[32]I have explored the place of Desnoes in revolutionary Cuban literature and the reasons for his success in more detail in "Edmundo Desnoes and Cuba's Lost Generation," *Latin American Research Review*, 12.3 (1977), 129-135.

but live on the fringe in total social isolation. By choosing these "parasites" for his protagonists, Desnoes was able to accomplish the seemingly impossible: develop a strong conflict between highly-developed individuals and Cuban revolutionary society, even arousing reader sympathy for the individuals. He managed this by portraying the "gusanos" not as evil threats but as pathetic, rootless, and perhaps naive individuals who should either become involved in the revolution or go to another country where they could begin meaningful lives. Thus Desnoes was able to write individuations without posing a serious threat to the revolutionary society or to its leadership. Even so, Desnoes, like Solzhenitsyn, eventually fled to the United States.

There have been isolated examples within socialist countries of distinguished persons insisting on the need for social criticism and dissent. The venerable Lukács himself stressed the importance of critical realism within socialist societies: "Genuine Marxism . . . is based on the exploration of objective reality, it must be in the interests of Marxism to enter into a close alliance with critical realism" (*Contemporary Realism*, p. 108). Lukács did not accept that literature must offer positive values and solutions to problems, as has been the history of socialist realism: "It is sectarian to expect every criticism to be accompanied by a solution, or to be based exclusively on communist principles" (*Contemporary Realism*, p. 108). This point of view, although it has echoed sporadically through the Soviet Union and Cuba, has never prevailed, and is seldom even allowed public airing. Criticism is equated with counter-revolution, and is not tolerated.

Individuation, the primary form of the novel, cannot then be considered viable in strongly socialist countries. Moreover, in the West the dehumanization of society by large corporate structures, and by the increasing centralization of control, poses a serious threat to individualism as it is represented and defended in the genre. In general we seem to be witnessing a retreat from individualism and from freedom: "We have ceased in recent years to believe in the reality and authority, the concrete *factualness*, of individual experience--and it may even be that we have lost our ability to respond as we once did to the reality of a specific social situation."[33] This retreat has been accompanied by a corresponding increase in the importance of

---

[33] John W. Aldridge, Forward to *The Politics of Twentieth-Century Novelists*, ed. George A. Panichas (New York: Hawthorn Books, Inc., 1971), p. xiv.

material objects. Goldmann has observed that since 1912 the world has been increasingly characterized by the "gradual disappearance of the individual as an essential reality and, correlatively, by the increasing independence of objects . . . the human being has lost all essential reality either as an individual or as a community . . . ."[34] A shift of such dimension, even if it is not as total as Goldmann believes, has grave consequences for character as it has existed in the traditional novel.

Goldmann distinguishes in fiction two stages that reflect this transformation. The first is characterized by the replacement of the individual by the ideologies of socialism--community, institutions, etc.--replacements that result in epic literature. The second, more problematic from a generic perspective, "is characterized by an abandonment of any attempt to replace the problematic hero and individual biography by another reality and by the effort to write the novel of the absence of subject, of the non-existence of any ongoing search" (*Sociology of the Novel*, p. 13). The literature so described has, as yet, no clear identification with any particular genre, and may, perhaps, either be made up of works that fit into various traditional genres or may actually represent a new form that has not yet been clearly identified or studied. It is clearly not individuation.

Whether because human reality has been replaced by objective reality, as argued by Goldmann, or because both have been replaced by the reality of the imagination, as argued by Seltzer,[35] there is no longer room for the human personality or for the dialectical relationship between self and world, which is both a result of and a contribution to that personality. As in the literature in which the individual is totally isolated with no intercourse whatsoever with the world, which is also a strong impulse in contemporary literature, the traditional ingredients of individuation are missing: "This particular ideology [the incognito, man is totally isolated] was of cardinal importance; by destroying the complex tissue of man's relations with his environment, it furthered the dissolution of personality" (Lukács, *Contemporary Realism*, p. 28). Character as individual, as personality, has

---

[34] Lucien Goldmann, *Towards a Sociology of the Novel*, trans. Alan Sheridan (London: Tavistock Publications Limited, 1975), p. 138.

[35] Alvin J. Seltzer, *Chaos in the Novel--The Novel in Chaos* (New York: Shocken Books, 1974), p. 378.

thus tended to disappear from fiction, and where this has happened, the primary form of the novel has disappeared as well. However, as we shall see in the conclusion of this study, individuation may be in far less difficulty in terms of survival than is generally supposed.

CONCLUSION

There is a severe limitation to all argument and speculation concerning the recent past, the present, and the future of prose fiction. Theorists tend to treat fiction as a total body, and discuss it as if it should be the same in all parts of the world, when in fact they are dealing with only the fiction of Europe and perhaps the United States, or more probably that of France, England, occasionally Germany, and only infrequently that of Italy, Spain, Latin America or Africa. Thus when Latin American fiction suddenly gained world prominence, it was simply incorporated into the body of current world literature. There is certainly a great deal of validity in such an approach, but individuation itself is highly dependent on a number of extra-literary factors that are determined on a very local basis--a sense of cultural identity, a high regard for individualism, freedom to engage in social dissent, etc.--requisites that are only now being met in some societies and that may not be met for a long time in others. There are many countries in Latin America, Africa, and other parts of the world that do not yet have this literary form, and surely there are cultures in which it may never be possible.

Geoffrey Hartman's observation that "we still have not found a theory linking the form of the medium to the form of the artist's historical consciousness"[1] owes much of its validity to text-oriented critics' refusal to consider the artist's historical consciousness and the socially-oriented critics' corresponding refusal to engage the text on its formal level. Individuation is a literary form that is most properly approached as a genre that is inseparable from the *genius loci*. Many excellent critics have written on the political nature of literature without losing sight of the importance of aesthetics, but perhaps even these have inadequately judged the political spectrum available to the novelist.[2] Perhaps, despite the fact that the novel is generally viewed as the most flexible and "loose" of literary genres, its central form, individuation, is, in truth, less flexible than is supposed. Most literary genres can span a broad spectrum of political tastes. Individuations cannot. A conservative, "pro-state" individuation is as impossi-

---

[1] Geoffrey H. Hartman, *Beyond Formalism: Literary Essays 1958-1970* (New Haven and London: Yale University Press, 1970), p. 366.
[2] See especially the works of Raymond Williams and Eugene Goodheart.

ble as an anarchic one. In fact, the entire conservative to liberal range available to the individuator is rather narrow.

Those who would speak on "the novel," and, in related proclamations, on the "state of the world," or on "contemporary society," would do well to exercise more caution than is typical. Richard Brown's declarations on "The Position of the Narrative in Contemporary Society,"[3] in which he speaks of the disappearance of "a social order of meaning, a political economy and collective psychology, in which public action by moral agents was possible, in which a sense of lived connection between personal character and public conduct prevailed" (p. 545), are surely not valid for all corners of the world. The immense popularity of foreign novelists in countries that have traditionally been major producers and consumers of novels is due primarily to the fact that these authors work from within environments that supposedly, according to the western experts, no longer exist.

There is a good deal of cultural arrogance reflected by those who speak of the disintegration of society as if it were a universal truth. Even Gerald Graff, who is far more careful than most critics when they address this subject, believes the "classic novel" (individuation) has disappeared because society has become so diffuse and ill-defined since World War II that it does not serve well as a backdrop against which to illuminate the individual.[4] Such arguments are simply untrue when one looks beyond Europe and the United States. Even the hypothesis that the traditional centers of the novel can no longer produce individuations may be false, or only temporarily valid, for the circumstances that are conducive to such literary activity may appear and disappear with very little warning. At times, the sudden appearance of a single or a group of individuations is the best sign that indeed such a moment has come, and may even have already gone. No matter what the current situation may be in the United States, or England, or France, individuations are as common on bookstore shelves as ever. Even in England John Fowles and Graham Greene kept the tradition alive long after its supposed death. And, it is often

---

[3] Richard Harvey Brown, "The Position of the Narrative in Contemporary Society," *New Literary History*, 11.3 (Spring 1980), 545-550.

[4] Gerald Graff, *Literature Against Itself: Literary Ideas in Modern Society* (Chicago and London: University of Chicago Press, 1979). See especially "Babbitt at the Abyss," pp. 207-239.

the power and fascination of their individuations, not anthropological curiosity about life in their countries, that has made third world authors so successful internationally.

None of this is to say that when individuations emerge in a given region they are not strongly influenced by or do not become a part of world fiction as we understand it. Indeed, the sudden excellence of the form on a national or regional basis may, because of resulting international prominence, result in a rather short life. To a degree, such has been the case of Latin American fiction. The "Boom" brought forth for the first time a substantial number of individuations that were worthy of international recognition on the basis of the excellence of their literary quality. Sudden acclaim brought superb writers--Donoso, García Márquez, Fuentes, Carpentier, Vargas Llosa, Cortázar, Borges, Cabrera Infante, and many others--into contact with each other and with the literary circles of the United States and Europe, with the result that many of those who were at first individuators became expert practitioners of "new fiction" in an international sense, and turned away, at least temporarily, from individuation.

Thus it is almost impossible to engage in any meaningful speculation concerning the future of individuation on a world scale. We may anticipate that in nations that have been under strong repressive governments for a long period of time, the form may, as governments fall, become extremely important. How long it endures will depend largely on the characteristics of the new society and the new government. In the case of Cuba, the duration was quite short because the right-wing dictatorship was replaced by a strong socialist dictatorship, which even in its early years allowed only novels that were critical of the earlier regime, a theme that was soon exhausted and became irrelevant with the passage of time. Concern with the problems of the new society was not permitted and individuation quickly disappeared.

International or world fiction can be discussed with more assurance than can individuation, for it reveals a number of distinguishable patterns and characteristics. One of the most prominent features of fiction has been the replacement of human complexity with cerebral complexity, a trend that is clearly manifested in detective stories, labyrinths, and intellectual puzzles:

> The detective novel is day by day moving further away from the novel, that is to say from the portrayal of life and passions, in order to approach the nature of pure problems in which one glides smoothly from the statement to the solution. The qualities demanded are more and more of a mathematical nature. Reasoning eliminates sensation.[5]

This trend has been accompanied by a strong tendency to view literature and its study as scientific endeavors. The scientific approach to literature, as typified by structuralism, semiotics, deconstruction and other movements, has removed literature an additional step from life and from what has traditionally been considered art: "The introduction of manipulated symbolism into the theory and practice of literary language inevitably produces a false polarization because of the inherent tendency of signs to eliminate multidimensionality."[6] To a large degree the increasingly dry scientific nature of literature and literary study is a result of the rapid growth and increasing dominance of technology in our daily lives.

Detective fiction has always had a strong scientific base, incorporating the best of technology that was readily available and using deductive methods of scientific investigation. Thus it is hardly surprising that along with and out of detective fiction has come an even more technological literary form, science fiction: "Even popular literature appears to be slowly shifting its center of gravity from murder stories to science fiction . . . . [The setting of science fiction] is often of a kind that appears to us as technologically miraculous. It is thus a mode of romance . . . ."[7] Romance, myth, epic, satire, and the historical novel, are all trends that are much in evidence today. Robert Scholes has termed much of this literature "fabulation," an appropri-

----

[5]"La novela policial se aleja cada día más de la novela, es decir de la pintura de la vida y de las pasiones, para aproximarse a la naturaleza de un problema puro en donde uno se desliza suavemente del enunciado a la solución. Las cualidades que se le exigen son de carácter cada vez más matemática. El razonamiento elimina la sensación." Roger Caillois, *Sociología de la novela* (Buenos Aires: SUR, 1942), p. 62.

[6]Georgy Lukács, Preface to *Writer and Critic and Other Essays*, ed. and trans. Arthur D. Kahn (New York: Grosset & Dunlap, 1970), p. 11.

[7]Northrop Frye, *Anatomy of Criticism: Four Essays* (New York: Atheneum, 1967), p. 49.

ate name for it removes the confusion inherent in attempting to subsume these tendencies under the term "novel," and while contemporary writers disagree on whether or not the novel is dead, their remarks clearly indicate that they do not consider it a propitious time, at least in world literature, for the "novel," by which they clearly mean that form we have called "individuation":

> The novel of characters belongs entirely to the past, it describes a period: that which marked the apogee of the individual. (Robbe-Grillet)

* * *

> What has died is not the novel, but precisely the bourgeois form of the novel and its point of reference, realism, which entails a descriptive and psychological style of observing individuals in personal and social relations. (Carlos Fuentes)

* * *

> ... pure romance really belongs to the future, which is absolutely cut off from any possible reference to truth of fact or truth of sensation. (Scholes and Kellogg)[8]

It would be not only foolish, but also inaccurate to conclude that individuation, except for sporadic outbursts in situations we have described, is dead as an international art form. The epic, the romance, and the serious, artistic historical novel have been declared dead, but are now more vital than ever. But we may have to wait a long while for the individuation to return to prominence in some coun-

----

[8] Alain Robbe-Grillet, *For a New Novel: Essays on Fiction*, trans. Richard Howard (New York: Grove Press Inc., 1965), p. 28; "Lo que ha muerto no es la novela, sino precisamente la forma burguesa de la novela y su término de referencia, el realismo, que supone un estilo descriptivo y sicológico de observar a individuos en relaciones personales y sociales." Carlos Fuentes, *La nueva novela* (México: Cuadernos de Joaquín Mortiz, 1969), p. 17; Robert Scholes and Robert Kellogg, *The Nature of Narrative* (London, Oxford, New York: Oxford University Press, 1968), p. 228.

tries, for it can return only if the individual as a full, psychological entity, of value in and of himself, returns to prominence, and if the social conditions we have described are again fully met.

Meanwhile, however, individuation has become increasingly important as a literary form in those areas where the novel clearly is not dead.[9] The Latin Americans are turning their talents more and more to its cultivation. Mario Vargas Llosa has produced a steady stream of individuations from *La ciudad y los perros* (1962, *The Time of the Hero*) to *Historia de Mayta* (1984 *The Real Life of Alejandro Mayta*). Gabriel García Márquez turned from the magical fabulations of *Cien años de soledad* (1967, *One Hundred Years of Solitude*) and *El otoño del patriarca* (1975, *The Autumn of the Patriarch*) to individuations, with *Crónica de una muerte anunciada* (1981, *Chronicle of a Death Foretold*) and *El amor en los tiempos del cólera* (1985, *Love in Times of Colera*). Carlos Fuentes, after early individuations, such as *La muerte de Artemio Cruz* (1962, *The Death of Artemio Cruz*), turned to more fabulous narrations, culminating with *Terra Nostra* (1975), but then turned again to mimesis and the psychology of characters in *Una familia lejana* (1980, *Distant Relations*). Individuation, as a genre, is but one possible form among many, and many authors who cultivate it do not do so to the exclusion of other forms. At present, individuation seems to be more alive than at any time in recent history, and there is good reason to believe that its prominence as a third world literary form is only beginning.

---

[9]Goodheart's discussion of Naipaul clearly places the Trinidadian author in the tradition of individuators. See Eugene E. Goodheart, "Naipaul and the Voices of Negation," *Salmagundi*, 54 (Fall 1981), 44-58.

BIBLIOGRAPHY

Alter, Robert. *Motives for Fiction*. Cambridge and London: Harvard University Press, 1984.

---. *Partial Magic*: *The Novel as a Self-Conscious Genre*. Berkeley and Los Angeles: University of California Press, 1975.

Ames, Van Meter. *Aesthetics of the Novel*. New York: Gordian Press Inc., 1966. First published Ann Arbor, Michigan: Edwards Brothers, Inc., 1928.

Auerbach, Erich. *Mimesis*: *The Representation of Reality in Western Literature*. Trans. Willard R. Trask. Princeton: Princeton University Press, 1968.

Bakhtin, M.M. *The Dialogic Imagination*: *Four Essays*. Trans. Caryl Emerson and Michael Holquist. Ed. Michael Holquist. Austin and London: University of Texas Press, 1981.

Barthes, Roland. *Image-Music-Text*. Trans. Stephen Heath. New York: Hill and Wang, 1977.

Bayley, John. *The Characters of Love*: *A Study in the Literature of Personality*. London: Constable and Company Ltd., 1960.

Bellamy, Joe David, ed. *The New Fiction*: *Interviews with Innovative American Writers*. Chicago: University of Illinois Press, 1974. Includes interviews with John Barth, Joyce Carol Oates, William H. Gass, Donald Barthelme, Ronald Sukenick, Tom Wolfe, John Hawkes, Susan Sontag, Ishmael Reed, Jerzy Kosinski, John Gardner, and Kurt Vonnegut Jr.

Benedetti, Mario. *El escritor latinoamericano y la revolución posible*. Buenos Aires: Editorial Alfa Argentina, 1974.

Benjamin, Walter. "The Storyteller: Reflections on the Works of Nikolai Leskov." In *Illuminations*. Trans. Harry Zohn. Ed. Hannah Arendt. New York: Harcourt, Brace & World, Inc., 1968.

Bergonzi, Bernard. *The Situation of the Novel*. London: Macmillan Press, Ltd., 1979.

Bernard, Jack F. *Up From Caesar: A Survey of the History of Italy from the Fall of the Roman Empire to the Collapse of Fascism.* Garden City: Doubleday & Company, Inc., 1970.

Bloom, Edward, ed. "In Defense of Authors and Readers." *Novel: A Forum on Fiction,* 11 (1977), 5-25. Panel discussion including Wayne C. Booth, Hyatt H. Waggoner, Frank Durand, Edward Bloom, Wolfgang Iser, Inge Crosman, Robert Crosman, and Roger Henkle.

Bloom, Harold, Paul de Man, Jaques Derrida, Geoffrey Hartman, and J. Hillis Miller. *Deconstruction and Criticism.* New York: The Seabury Press, 1979.

Booth, Wayne C. *The Rhetoric of Fiction.* Chicago: University of Chicago Press, 1961.

Bradbury, Malcolm. *Possibilities: Essays on the State of the Novel.* London: Oxford University Press, 1973.

---. "Towards a Poetics of Fiction: An Approach Through Structure." *Novel: A Forum on Fiction,* 1 (1967), 45-52.

Bremond, Claude. "The Logic of Narrative Possibilities." *New Literary History,* 11.3 (Spring 1980), 387-411.

Brown, Richard Harvey. "The Position of the Narrative in Contemporary Society." *New Literary History,* 11.3 (Spring 1980), 545-550.

Burg, David, and George Feifer. *Solzhenitsyn.* New York: Stein and Day/Publishers, 1972.

Caillois, Roger. *Sociología de la novela.* Buenos Aires: Sur, 1942.

Campbell, Joseph. *The Hero with a Thousand Faces.* Cleveland: World Publishing Company, 1956.

Carlyle, Thomas. *Carlyle: Selected Works, Reminiscences and Letters.* Ed. Julian Symons. Cambridge: Harvard University Press, 1970.

Castro, Fidel. *Fidel Castro.* Argentina: Cuadernos de La Linea, n.d.

Champigny, Robert. *Ontology of the Narrative: An Analysis.* The Hague, Paris: Mouton, 1972.

Chase, Richard. *The American Novel and its Tradition*. Garden City: Doubleday & Company, Inc., 1957.

Chatman, Seymour. *Story and Discourse*: *Narrative Structure in Fiction and Film*. Ithaca: Cornell University Press, 1978.

Clarkson, Jesse D. *A History of Russia*. 2nd ed. New York: Random House, 1969.

Clements, Robert J. and Joseph Gibaldi. *Anatomy of the Novella*: *The European Tale Collection From Boccaccio and Chaucer to Cervantes*. New York: New York University Press, 1977.

Coates, Paul. *The Realist Fantasy*: *Fiction and Reality Since Clarissa*. London: Macmillan, 1983.

Cohen, Ralph. "History and Genre." *New Literary History*, 17.2 (Winter 1986), 203-218.

Colby, Robert A. *Fiction with a Purpose*: *Major and Minor Nineteenth Century Novels*. Bloomington: Indiana University Press, 1967.

Collazos, Oscar, Julio Cortázar, and Mario Vargas Llosa. *Literatura en la revolución y revolución en la literatura*. 2nd ed. México: Siglo Veintiuno Editores, S.A., 1971.

Collins, R.G., ed. *The Novel and its Changing Form*. Winnepeg: University of Manitoba Press, 1972.

Colmer, John, ed. *Approaches to the Novel*. Adelaide, Australia: Rigby Limited, 1966.

Crawford, Francis Marion. *The Novel*: *What it Is*. 1893; rpt. Freeport, New York: Books for Libraries Press, 1969.

Culler, Jonathan. *A Structuralist Poetics*: *Structuralism, Linguistics and the Study of Literature*. Ithaca: Cornell University Press, 1975.

Davis, Walter A. *The Act of Interpretation*: *a Critique of Literary Reason*. Chicago: University of Chicago Press, 1978.

Donoso, José. *The Boom in Spanish American Literature*: *A Personal History*. New York: Columbia University Press, 1977.

Dostoyevsky, Fyodor. *The Brothers Karamazov*. Ed. Manuel Komroff. New York: Signet Books, 1958.

Edel, Leon. *The Modern Psychological Novel*. New York: Grove Press and Evergreen Books, 1955.

Fehér, Ferenc. "Is the Novel Problematic? A Contribution to the Theory of the Novel." *Telos*, 15 (1973), 47-74.

Felperin, Howard. *Beyond Deconstruction*: *The Uses and Abuses of Literary Theory*. Oxford: Clarendon Press, 1985.

Forster, E.M. *Aspects of the Novel*. New York: Harcourt, Brace & World, Inc., 1927.

Foucault, Michel. *The Order of Things*: *An Archaeology of the Human Sciences*. New York: Pantheon Books, 1970.

Fowler, Alastair. *Kinds of Literature*: *An Introduction to the Theory of Genres and Modes*. Cambridge: Harvard University Press, 1982.

Frank, Joseph. *The Widening Gyre*. New Brunswick: Rutgers University Press, 1963.

Freud, Sigmund. *A General Introduction to Psychoanalysis*. Trans. Joan Riviere. New York: Simon & Schuster, Inc. Pocket Book, 1960.

Friedman, Alan. *The Turn of the Novel*: *The Transition to Modern Fiction*. London, Oxford, New York: Oxford University Press, 1966.

Friedman, Norman. "Point of View in Fiction: The Development of a Critical Concept." *PMLA*, 60 (1955), 1160-84.

Fromm, Erich. *Escape from Freedom*. New York: Holt, Rinehart and Winston, 1941.

---. *The Sane Society*. New York: Rinehart & Company, Inc., 1955.

Frye, Northrup. *Anatomy of Criticism: Four Essays*. New York: Atheneum, 1967.

---. *Fables of Identity: Studies in Poetic Mythology*. New York: Harcourt, Brace & World, Inc., 1963.

Fuentes, Carlos. *La nueva novela hispanoamericana*. México: Cuadernos de Joaquín Mortiz, 1969.

Gass, William H. *Fiction and the Figures of Life*. New York: Alfred A. Knopf, 1970.

Girard, René. *Deceit, Desire, and the Novel: Self and Other in Literary Structure*. Trans. Yvonne Freccero. Baltimore: The John Hopkins Press, 1965.

Goldmann, Lucien. *Towards a Sociology of the Novel*. Trans. Alan Sheridan. London: Tavistock Publications Limited, 1975.

Goodheart, Eugene E. "Naipaul and the Voices of Negation." *Salmagundi*, 54 (Fall 1981), 44-58.

---. *The Skeptic Disposition in Contemporary Criticism*. Princeton: Princeton University Press, 1984.

Goodman, Paul. *The Structure of Literature*. Chicago: University of Chicago Press, 1954.

Graff, Gerald. *Literature Against Itself: Literary Ideas in Modern Society*. Chicago and London: University of Chicago Press, 1979.

Grossvogel, David I. *Limits of the Novel: Evolutions of a Form from Chaucer to Robbe-Grillet*. Ithaca: Cornell University Press, 1968.

Guillén, Claudio. *Literature as System: Essays Toward the Theory of Literary History*. Princeton: Princeton University Press, 1971.

Hägg, Thomas. *The Novel in Antiquity*. Berkeley and Los Angeles: University of California Press, 1983.

Haines, Helen Elizabeth. *What's in a Novel*. New York: Columbia University Press, 1942.

Halperin, John, ed. *The Theory of the Novel: New Essays*. New York: Oxford University Press, 1974.

Hamilton, Clayton Meeker. *The Art of Fiction: A Formulation of its Fundamental Principles*. New York: Doubleday, Doran & Company, Inc., 1939.

Hardy, Barbara. *The Appropriate Form: An Essay on the Novel*. London: The Athlone Press, 1964.

Hartman, Geoffrey H. *Beyond Formalism: Literary Essays 1958-1970*. New Haven and London: Yale University Press, 1970.

---. *Saving the Text: Literature/Derrida/Philosophy*. Baltimore and London: The Johns Hopkins University Press, 1981.

Harvey, William John. *Character and the Novel*. Ithaca: Cornell University Press, 1965.

Hauser, Arnold. *The Social History of Art*. 2 vols. New York: Alfred A. Knopf, 1952.

Hawkes, Terence. *Structuralism & Semiotics*. Berkeley and Los Angeles: University of California Press, 1977.

Hegel, G.W.F. *Aesthetics*. Trans. T.M. Knox. Oxford: Oxford University Press, 1975.

Heiserman, Arthur. *The Novel Before the Novel: Essays and Discussions about the Beginnings of Prose Fiction in the West*. Chicago and London: University of Chicago Press, 1977.

Hirsch, E.D. Jr. *Validity in Interpretation*. New Haven and London: Yale University Press, 1967.

Holland, Norman N. *The Dynamics of Literary Response*. New York: Oxford University Press, 1968.

Holquist, Michael, and Walter Reed. "Six Theses on the Novel--and Some Metaphors." *New Literary History*, 11.3 (Spring 1980), 413-423.

Howe, Susanne. *Novels of Empire*. New York: Columbia University Press, 1949.

Humphrey, Robert. *Stream of Consciousness in the Modern Novel*. Berkeley and Los Angeles: University of California Press, 1965.

Hutchens, Eleanor N., "Towards a Poetics of Fiction: The Novel as Cronomorph." *Novel: A Forum on Fiction*, 5 (1972), 215-224.

Hynes, Samuel. "The Whole Contention Between Mr. Bennett and Mrs. Woolf." *Novel: A Forum on Fiction*, 1 (1967), 34-44.

Iser, Wolfgang. *The Act of Reading: A Theory of Aesthetic Response*. Baltimore: Johns Hopkins Press, 1978.

James, Henry. *The Art of Fiction and Other Essays*. New York: Oxford University Press, 1948.

Kermode, Frank. *The Sense of an Ending*. New York: Oxford University Press, 1968.

Kestner, Joseph A. *The Spatiality of the Novel*. Detroit: Wayne State University Press, 1978.

Knight, Everett. *A Theory of the Classical Novel*. New York: Barnes & Noble, Inc., 1970.

Lanser, Susan Sniader. *The Narrative Act: Point of View in Prose Fiction*. Princeton: Princeton University Press, 1981.

Larson, Charles L. *The Novel in the Third World*. Washington: Inscape, 1976.

Lawrence, D.H., "Morality and the Novel." *The Calendar of Modern Letters*, 2 (1925), 269-274.

Lerner, Lawrence. *The Truth-Tellers: Jane Austen, George Eliot, D.H. Lawrence*. New York: Schocken Books, Inc., 1967.

Lesser, Simon O. *Fiction and the Unconscious*. Boston: Beacon Press, 1957.

Levin, Harry. *The Gates of Horn: A Study of Five French Realists*. New York: Oxford University Press, 1963.

Lodge, David. *The Novelist at the Crossroads and Other Essays on Fiction and Criticism*. Ithaca: Cornell University Press, 1971.

Lubbock, Percy. *The Craft of Fiction*. New York: The Viking Press, 1957.

Lukács, Georgy. *The Historical Novel*. Trans. Hannah and Stanley Mitchell. London: Merlin Press, 1962.

---. *History and Class Consciousness: Studies in Marxist Dialectics*. Trans. Rodney Livingstone. Cambridge: The MIT Press, 1971.

---. *The Meaning of Contemporary Realism*. Trans. John and Necke Mander. London: Merlin Press, 1963.

---. *Realism in Our Time: Literature and the Class Struggle*. New York: Harper & Row, 1964.

---. *Studies in European Realism: A Sociological Survey of the Writings of Balzac, Stendhal, Zola, Tolstoy, Gorki, and Others*. Trans. Edith Bone. London: Hillway Publishing Co., 1950.

---. *The Theory of the Novel*. Trans. Anna Bostock. Cambridge: The MIT Press, 1971.

---. *Writer & Critic and Other Essays*. Ed. and trans. Arthur D. Kahn. New York: Grosset & Dunlap, 1970.

Lukes, Stephen. "Types of Individualism." In *Dictionary of the History of Ideas: Studies of Selected Pivotal Ideas*, Vol. II. Ed. Philip P. Wiener. New York: Charles Scribner's Sons, 1973, pp. 594-601.

MacAdam, Alfred J. *Modern Latin American Narratives: The Dreams of Reason*. Chicago: University of Chicago Press, 1977.

McCarthy, Mary. "The Fact in Fiction." *Partisan Review*, 27 (1960), 438-58.

McCormick, John. *Fiction as Knowledge; the Modern Post-Romantic Novel*. New Brunswick: Rutgers University Press, 1975.

Mallea, Eduardo. *Poderío de la novela*. Buenos Aires: Aguilar, 1965.

Malraux, André. Preface to *Days of Wrath*. Trans. Haakon M. Chevalier. New York: Random House, 1936.

Mao Tse-Tung. *Problems of Art and Literature*. New York: International Publishers, 1950.

Marx, Karl. *Economic and Philosophical Manuscripts of 1844*. In Karl Marx and Frederick Engels, *Collected Works*, Vol. III. London: Lawrence & Wishart, 1975.

Mendilow, A.A. *Time and the Novel*. New York: Humanities Press, 1965.

Meyerhoff, Hans. *Time in Literature*. Berkeley: University of California Press, 1956.

Miles, David H. "Portrait of the Marxist as a Young Hegelian: Lukács' *Theory of the Novel*." *PMLA*, 94 (1979), 22-35.

Miller, James Edwin, ed. *Myth and Method: Modern Theories of Fiction*. n.p.: University of Nebraska Press, 1960.

Mills, Nicolaus. "American Fiction and the Genre Critics." *Novel: A Forum on Fiction*, 2 (1969), 112-122.

Monroe, N. Elizabeth. *The Novel and Society: A Critical Study of the Modern Novel*. Chapel Hill: The University of North Carolina Press, 1941.

Muir, Edwin. *The Structure of the Novel*. New York: Harcourt, Brace and Company, 1929.

Nin, Anaïs. *The Novel of the Future*. New York: The Macmillan Company, 1968.

Ortega y Gassett, José. *The Dehumanization of Art and Other Writings on Art and Culture*. Trans. Willard Trask. Garden City: Doubleday & Company, Inc., 1956.

---. *Meditations on Quixote*. Trans. Evelyn Rugg and Diego Marín. New York: W.W. Norton & Company, Inc., 1963.

Orwell, George. *A Collection of Essays by George Orwell*. New York: Harcourt Brace Jovanovich, Inc., 1953.

Panichas, George A., ed. *The Politics of Twentieth-Century Novelists*. New York. Hawthorn Books, Inc., 1971.

Paris, Bernard J. "Form, Theme, and Imitation in Realistic Fiction." *Novel: A Forum on Fiction*, 1 (1968), 140-149.

Paterson, John. *The Novel as Faith: The Gospel According to James, Hardy, Conrad, Joyce, Lawrence and Virginia Woolf.* Boston: Gambit Inc., 1973.

Pearce, Roy Harvey, ed. *Experience in the Novel: Selected Papers from the English Institute.* New York: Columbia University Press, 1968.

Peavler, Terry J. "Edmundo Desnoes and Cuba's Lost Generation." *Latin American Research Review*, 12.3 (1977), 129-135.

The Poem of the Cid. Trans. W.S. Merwin, in *Medieval Epics*. New York: The Modern Library, n.d., pp. 441-590.

Poema de Mio Cid. Ed. Ramón Menéndez Pidal. Madrid: Espasa-Calpe, S.A., 1966.

Reed, Walter L. "The Problem with a Poetics of the Novel." *Novel: A Forum on Fiction*, 9 (1976), 101-113.

Reeve, Clara. *The Progress of Romance and the History of Charoba, Queen of Aegypt.* 1785; rpt. New York: The Facsimile Text Society, 1930.

Reichert, John. *Making Sense of Literature.* Chicago: University of Chicago Press, 1978.

Richards, I.A. *Principles of Literary Criticism.* London: Routledge & Kegan Paul Ltd., 1960.

Robbe-Grillet, Alain. *For a New Novel: Essays on Fiction.* Trans. Richard Howard. New York: Grove Press Inc., 1965.

Sale, Roger, ed. *Discussions of the Novel.* Boston: D.C. Heath and Company, 1960.

Sammons, Jeffrey L. *Literary Sociology and Practical Criticism.* Bloomington: Indiana University Press, 1977.

Sánchez Vázquez, Adolfo. *Estética y marxismo.* 2 vols. México: Ediciones Era, 1970.

---. *Las ideas estéticas de Marx.* Havana: Instituto Cubano del Libro, 1973.

Scholes, Robert, ed. *Approaches to the Novel: Materials for a Poetics*. 2nd ed. San Francisco: Chandler Publishing Co., 1966.

---. *Fabulation and Metafiction*. Urbana, Chicago, London: University of Illinois Press, 1979.

---. *The Fabulators*. New York: Oxford University Press, 1967.

---. *Structuralism in Literature: An Introduction*. New Haven and London: Yale University Press, 1974.

---. "Towards a Poetics of Fiction: An Approach through Genre." *Novel: A Forum on Fiction*, 2 (1969), 101-111.

---. and Robert Kellogg. *The Nature of Narrative*. London, Oxford, New York: Oxford University Press, 1968.

Seltzer, Alvin J. *Chaos in the Novel--The Novel in Chaos*. New York: Schocken Books, 1974.

Simenon, Georges. *The Novel of Man*. Trans. Bernard Frechtman. New York: Harcourt, Brace & World, Inc., 1964.

Simms, William Gilmore. Prefatory note to *The Yemasse*. New York: American Book Company, 1937.

Slonim, Marc. *The Epic of Russian Literature: From its Origens through Tolstoy*. New York: Oxford University Press, 1950.

Smith, Rhea Marsh. *Spain: A Modern History*. Ann Arbor: University of Michigan Press, 1965.

Solzhenitsyn, Alexander. *Cancer Ward*. Trans. Nicholas Bethell and David Burg. New York: Farrar, Strauss and Giroux, 1969.

Spearman, Diana. *The Novel and Society*. London: Routledge and Kegan Paul, 1966.

Spilka, Mark, ed. "Character as a Lost Cause." *Novel: A Forum on Fiction*, 11 (1978), 197-217. Discussion between Spilka, Martin Price, Julian Moynahan and Arnold Weinstein.

---., ed. *Towards a Poetics of Fiction*. Bloomington: Indiana University Press, 1977. Collection of articles by the same title from *Novel: A Forum on Fiction*.

Stang, Richard. *The Theory of the Novel in England: 1850-1870*. New York: Columbia University Press, 1959.

Stevik, Philip, ed. *The Theory of the Novel*. New York: The Free Press, 1967.

Surmelian, Leon. *Techniques of Fiction Writing: Measure and Madness*. New York: Doubleday & Company, Inc., 1969.

Swingewood, Alan. *The Novel and Revolution*. Great Britain: Barnes & Noble, 1975.

Tillyard, E.M.W. *The Epic Strain in the English Novel*. Fair Lawn, New Jersey: Essential Books, Inc., 1958.

Tobin, Patricia Derchsel. *Time and the Novel: The Genealogical Imperative*. Princeton: Princeton University Press, 1978.

Todorov, Tzvetan. *Introduction to Poetics*. Trans. Richard Howard. Minneapolis: University of Minnesota Press, 1981.

---. "The Origen of Genres." *New Literary History*, 8.1 (Autumn 1976), 159-170.

---. *The Poetics of Prose*. Trans. Richard Howard. Ithaca: Cornell University Press, 1977.

Toliver, Harold. *Animate Illusions; Explorations of Narrative Structure*. Lincoln: University of Nebraska, 1974.

Tolstoi, Leo. *War and Peace*. Trans. Louise and Aylmer Maude. Ed. George Gibian. New York: W.W. Norton & Company, Inc., 1966.

Trollope, Anthony. *An Autobiography*. Berkeley and Los Angeles: University of California Press, 1947.

Trotsky, Leon. *Literature and Revolution*. Trans. Rose Strunsky. Ann Arbor: University of Michigan Press, 1960.

Turnell, Martin. *The Novel in France*. New York: Vintage Books, 1958.

Vargas Llosa, Mario. *García Márquez*: *Historia de un deicidio*. Barcelona: Barral Editores, S.A., 1971.

Vicens Vives, Jaime. *Approaches to the History of Spain*. Trans. Joan Connelly Ullman. Berkeley and Los Angeles: University of California Press, 1967.

Visser, N.W. "The Generic Identity of the Novel." *Novel: A Forum on Fiction*, 11 (1978), 101-114.

Wagner, Geoffrey. *Five for Freedom: A Study of Feminism in Fiction*. Rutherford, Madison, Teaneck: Farleigh Dickenson University Press, 1973.

Ward, Wilfrid Philip. *Last Lectures by Wilfrid Ward*. 1918; rpt. Freeport, N.Y.: Books for Libraries Press, Inc., 1967.

Watt, Ian. *The Rise of the Novel: Studies in Defoe, Richardson and Fielding*. Berkeley and Los Angeles: University of California Press, 1967.

Weismann, Robert. *Structure and Society in Literary History: Studies in the History and Theory of Historical Criticism*. Charlottesville: University Press of Virginia, 1976.

Wellek, René, and Austin Warren. *Theory of Literature*. 3rd ed. New York: Harcourt, Brace & World, Inc., 1962.

West, Paul. *The Modern Novel*. 2 vols. London: Hutchinson University Library, 1965.

Wilkins, Ernest Hatch, and Thomas G. Bergin. *A History of Italian Literature*. Cambridge: Harvard University Press, 1974.

Williams, Ioan, ed. *Novel and Romance 1700-1800: A Documentary Record*. New York: Barnes & Noble, Inc., 1970.

Williams, Raymond. *Culture and Society 1780-1950*. Harmondsworth, Middlesex: Penguin Books Ltd., 1961.

---. *The English Novel from Dickens to Lawrence*. New York: Oxford University Press, 1970.

---. *The Long Revolution*. New York: Columbia University Press, 1961.

---. *Marxism and Literature*. Oxford: Oxford University Press, 1977.

Wilson, Edmund. *Axel's Castle*. New York: Charles Scribner's Sons, 1959.

Woolf, Virginia. *The Common Reader*. New York: Harcourt, Brace and Company, 1925.

Wright, Austin M. *The Formal Principle in the Novel*. Ithaca: Cornell University Press, 1982.

INDEX

Absalom, Absalom!...26
Aeneid, The...2, 17-18, 21
aesthetics
    and socialism...118
Aldridge, John W.
    on retreat from individualism...124
Alter, Robert
    on mimesis and the novel...35
    on realism...7
    on self-conscious novel...13
Amor en los tiempos del cólera, El...132
Auerbach, Erich...15, 96
    on character...33
    on individual and society...63
    on individualism and liberalism...69
    on novel in France and England...70
    on realism...83
    on Stendahl...95
Austen, Jane...55, 81, 90
Autumn of the Patriarch, The...132
Azuela, Mariano...17

Bakhtin, M.M....21
    Dialogic Imagination, The...xiii
    heteroglossia...xiv
    on defining the novel...1
    on novel as genre...xiii
Barral, Carlos
    contribution to the *Boom*...112
Barthes, John
    on living persons as characters...93
Barthes, Roland...7
    on narrative analysis...29
    on realism...6
Batista, Fulgencio...110-111
Benedetti, Mario
    on art and revolution...120
Benjamin, Walter
    on novel and isolation...13
Bennett, Arnold
    on novelist as dissident...87-88
Bergonzi, Bernard...2
Bernard, Jack F.
    on history of Italy...111
Bleak House...96
Böhl von Faber, Cecilia...82
Booth, Wayne C.
    on character...34
    on character and reader...53-55
    on realism versus aesthetic purity...5
Borges, Jorge Luis...98, 129
Bradbury, Malcolm
    on novel theory...3
Bremond, Claude...40
Brothers Karamazov, The...95, 97
Brown, Richard H.
    on disintegration of society...128

Cabrera Infante, Guillermo...98, 110, 129
Caillois, Roger
    on detective fiction...130
Campbell, Joseph
    on heroism...76
    on individual and society...48, 76
Capote, Truman...98
Carlyle, Thomas
    on social upheaval...69
Carpentier, Alejo...56, 110, 129
    and the problem of verisimilitude...8
Castro, Fidel...110-111
    on art and politics...119
    on freedom...117
Cela, Camilo José...73
Celestina, La...104

Cervantes, Miguel de...27, 53, 104-106
character...4, 9-12, 14-16, 18, 20, 25, 31, 44-46, 48, 51, 53, 71, 107, 125, 131
   and author...52, 82, 92, 100
   and impotence...98
   and mimesis...36
   and plot...45
   and reader...53-55
   and society...37-38, 43
   and structuralism...35
   authorial control...14, 35
   change...46-47
   illustrative...19-20
   reader identification...54-55, 82
   representational...19
   symbolic...20
   types...32-39, 59-61
Chase, Richard
   on character versus plot...108
   on novel versus romance...20
Chronicle of a Death Foretold...132
Cien años de soledad...132
Ciudad y los perros, La...132
Cofiño López, Manuel...121
Cohen, Ralph...xiii
conflict...4, 12, 20-21, 24, 39, 41-49, 60, 62, 66-67, 69, 71-72, 75, 79-80, 83, 85-87, 92, 98, 100
   and endings...47, 49
   types...40
Cortázar, Julio...129
Cossío Woodward, Miguel...121
Crónica de una muerte anunciada...132
Culler, Jonathan
   on character and conflict...12
   on generic expectations...2
   on structuralism and the analysis of character...35
Cullman, Oscar...9

Day in the Life of Ivan Denisovich, A...122
Death in Venice...52
Death of Artemio Cruz, The...49, 132
Death of Ivan Ilyich, The...49
deconstruction
   and novel theory...xii
Defoe, Daniel...32
Derrida, Jacques...xiii
Desnoes, Edmundo...122-124
Dickens, Charles...37, 46, 51, 55, 96
Distant Relations...132
Doña Bárbara...23, 52
Don Quixote...15, 42, 47, 79, 94-95, 97-98, 104-105
Donoso, José...129
   on novel in Spanish America...100, 112
   on regionalism...83
Dostoewski, Fyodor...95

Edel, Leon...81
   on the subjective novel...97
epic...130-131
epic versus romance...21

Facundo...23
Faulkner, William...26, 92
Fehér, Ferenc
   on capitalism and the novel...71
   on character and conflict...45
   on freedom in the novel...15
   on novel versus epic...71
   on values...14
Felperin, Howard...xiv
   Beyond Deconstruction...xii
fiction
   as defense...93
   detective...129-130
   Europe versus Third World...127
   history of...127
   in the New World...108
   international...129-130

Fielding, Henry...34, 44
   on epic...100
Fischer, Ernst
   on two kinds of realism...114
Flaubert, Gustav...20, 50, 52
formalism...ix-x
Forster, E.M....45
   novel definition...3
   on plot types...46
Fowler, Alastair
   on genres and subgenres...25
   on need for theory of novel...xi
   on novel as genre...x
   on the picaresque...24-25
Fowles, John...27, 128
freedom
   and socialism...115
   as burden...74
   price of...66
   retreat from...75
Friedman, Alan
   on character and conflict...42
   on character and reader...53-54
   on character development...46
   on structure...57
Fromm, Erich
   Escape From Freedom...xi
   on failure of individualism...75
   on freedom...61-62
   on freedom as burden...74
   on individual as rebel...110
   on individualism...65
   on individuation...xi
   on price of freedom...66
   on retreat from individualism...72
Frye, Northrop...47, 75
   on character...20
   on character and conflict...12, 41
   on decline of the hero...96
   on Dickens...36
   on novelist and society...108
   on romance...24

   on science fiction...130
Fuentes, Carlos...129, 132
   on death of the bourgeois novel...131
   on novel in Spanish America...107
   on novelist as dissident...88
   on Spanish American novel...90

Gallegos, Rómulo...23
Gama, Vasco da...21
García Márquez, Gabriel...27, 129, 132
genre
   and national development...22
Girard, René
   on conflict in the novel...86
Goldmann, Lucien
   on history of the novel...67
   on modern social conditions...101
   on novel as defense...93
   on problematic individual...68-69
   on problematic individual and conflict...89
   on reification...75
   on retreat from individualism...125
Goodheart, Eugene...127
   on Naipaul...132
   Skeptic Disposition, The...xii
Goodman, Paul
   on epic...17-18
Graff, Gerald
   Literature Against Itself...xii
   on belief, truth, and reality...xii-xiii
   on disintegration of society...128
Great Expectations...36, 46, 55, 96
Greene, Graham...95, 128
   on novelist as dissident...94
Guillén, Claudio
   on the picaresque...24

Hägg, Thomas...1
Hamilton, Clayton Meeker
   on character...39
   on character and verisimilitude...34
   on novel versus epic...16-17
Harding, D.W.
   on Jane Austen...90
Hardy, Barbara
   on aesthetics...57
   on types of novels...25
Hartman, Geoffrey
   Beyond Formalism...xii
   on genre theory and historical consciousness...127
   Saving the Text...xii
Harvey, William J.
   on balance of conflict...43
   on character...9
   on character interrelationships...37
   on character types...32-33
   on characters and reality...34
   on novelist and society...103
Hauser, Arnold
   on conflict in the novel...85
   on Ibsen...72
   on Julien Sorel...90
   on rise of the novel...85
   on Samuel Richardson...80
   on time in the novel...8
Hawkes, John
   on the novel as criminal act...91
Hawks, Terence
   on novel as genre...x
Hawthorne, Nathaniel...18
Hegel, G.W.F.
   on character...71-72
   on conflict in the novel...86
   on individual...63
   on individualism...65
   on virtue and the individual...62
Heiserman, Arthur...1

hero
   decline of...96
Hirsch, E.D.
   on genres...2-3
Historia de Mayta...132
historical novel...130
Holquist, Michael and Walter Reed
   on conflict...11
   on dialectical nature of novel...13
Howe, Susanne...17
   on Australian literature...108-109

In Cold Blood...98
individual
   as character...93
   as rebel...110
   concept of...59
   freedom of...61, 117
individualism
   and capitalism...65, 67
   and Christianity...64
   and Reformation...65
   and socialism...73
   and totalitarianism...72-73
   failure of...75
   in England...64
   in France...64
   in Germany...64
   in Spanish America...100
   in United States...64
   retreat from...72, 76, 112, 124-125
individuation...xi-xii, 10-12, 20-21
   amorphous nature...70
   and ambiguity...90, 97
   and authoritarianism...110-112, 123
   and bourgeoisie...89
   and capitalism...70, 113-114, 120-121
   and colonialism...108-109
   and community...109, 113

and complexity...93
and dehumanization...124
and dissent...30, 50, 56, 79, 86, 92, 97-99, 103, 109, 113-114, 120
and female perspective...81
and freedom...97
and frontier...108
and heroes...76
and ideology...115, 120, 125, 127
and individualism...63, 79
and Industrial Revolution...67-69
and liberalism...69, 79
and mimesis...90
and modernism...97
and nationalism...106
and naturalism...99
and perspective...83
and politics...127-128
and press...111-112
and psychology...81
and reader recognition...51
and realism...69-70, 79
and reality...93
and revolution...87, 106
and romanticism...69-70, 79
and socialism...73-74, 113-122, 124
and socialist realism...114, 120-121
and society...28, 30, 110, 129, 132
and Third World...128-129
and traditional novel...88
and women...80
as dissent...110
as exploration...52-53, 100
character in...44
conservative nature of...89-90
definition...29
dialectical nature of...86-87, 89
disappearance of...125-126

genius loci...127
in Brazil...107
in Cuba...110-112, 121-124, 129
in England...109
in Europe and the U.S....128
in France...109
in Germany...109-110
in Italy...111
in Italy versus Cuba...111
in Latin America...107-108, 129, 132
in Russia...109, 111-112, 121-124
in Spain...73, 104-106, 111
in Spanish America...83-84, 90, 107, 112
liberal nature of...89-90
rise of...85
versus epic...21-22, 37, 47, 71, 93, 96, 110, 113-114, 121
versus fabulation...26
versus picaresque...41-42
versus romance...20-22, 47
individuator
as dissident...87-89, 91, 94, 103, 120, 124
causes of rebellion...92
survival of...101, 120

James, Henry...33, 44, 81, 98
on character...9-10
on character and society...31
on women and the novel...82
Joyce, James...26, 51, 56

Kermode, Frank
on time...9
Khrushchev, Nikita...122
Knight, Everett
on classical novel...88
on dual nature of the novelist...89
Kosinski, Jerzy

on conflict in the novel...86-87
on individual and society...75

Laforet, Carmen...73
Lazarillo de Tormes...104
Lévi-Strauss, Claude...x
Lenin, V.I.
    on literature and communism...117
Levin, Harry
    on character and the novel...31
    on French novel...70
    on German novel...109
    on history of genres...27
    on novel as parody...98
Lezama Lima, José...110
literature
    scientific approaches...130
Lodge, David...94
    on American literature...108
    on realism and liberalism...69
    on structure...56
    on *Tom Jones*...49
Los de abajo...90
Love in Times of Cholera...132
Lu Ting-Li...117
    on freedom...116
Lubbock, Percy...33, 44
    on character and conflict...46
Lukács, Georgy...66, 101, 122
    on author's vision...52
    on authorial control...130
    on character...10
    on character and conflict...41, 45
    on character types...33
    on conflict...67
    on conflict in the novel...86
    on critical realism...124
    on criticism and capitalism...113
    on Dickens...96
    on epic heroes...60
    on freedom...115
    on isolation of the individual...125
    on later European realists...50
    on literature under Stalin...121
    on novel and society...114
    on novel as dissent...95
    on novel versus epic...15-16
    on realism and capitalism...70
    on revolutionary romanticism...122
    on Tolstoy...94
    on transplanted Europeans...107
Lukes, Stephen
    on history of individualism...64
Lunacharsky, Anatoli
    on art and politics...119

Madame Bovary...20, 50, 52
Magic Mountain, The...97
Mallea, Eduardo...94
    on characters and authors...34
Malraux, Andre
    on individual and society...39
Mann, Thomas...52
Mao Tse-Tung
    on art and communism...117-118
    on art and politics...118
    on art as weapon...120
    on Marxism and creativity...115-116
Marsh, John...9
Martín Santos, Luis...73
McCarthy, Mary...8
    on epic and novel...38
Memories of Underdevelopment...123
Miles, David H....39
Mill, John Stewart
    and individualism...64
Miller, J. Hillis
    on the rise of the novel...85
mimesis...11, 31, 46-47, 50-51
Mist...98
mixed genres...22-24

Muerte de Artemio Cruz, La...132
Muir, Edwin
   on plot types...46
myth...130

naturalism
   and social realism...100
   in Spanish America...100
New Criticism...xii
Niebla...98
Norris, Frank...50, 52
novel
   and economic factors...76
   and individual...80
   and search for meaning...101
   and socialism...17
   and solitude...13
   and time...8
   and Utopia...108
   and women...80
   as deicide...91
   as dissent...13
   as exploration...101
   as genre...x, xiii, 131
   as *langue*...x
   as *parole*...x
   as propaganda...99
   as revenge...91
   death of...128, 131-132
   definition...1-3
   epistolary...82
   generic expectations...4
   history of...127
   in England versus Spanish America...84
   in Spanish America...107
   in U.S. versus Spanish America...107
   instability of...100
   provincial...83
   psychological...10
   types...44
   versus epic...xiii, 14-19, 26, 38-39, 49, 81, 100
   versus picaresque...xiii, 24-25
   versus romance...xiii, 14, 18-20, 26
   versus satire...26
novelist
   and social message...94
   as God...98
   as rebel...91
   uncertainty of...101

Odyssey, The...2, 8-9, 17-18, 21
One Hundred Years of Solitude...132
Ortega y Gasset, José
   on character...53
   on novel versus epic...15
Orwell, George...46
   on novelist and society...103, 112
Otoño del patriarca, El...132

Pardo Bazán, Emilia...82
Paris, Bernard J.
   on time...11
Pedro Páramo...26
perspective...52, 55
pietas...62
plot types...46
Poema de mio Cid, El...21, 47
Portrait of the Artist as a Young Man, A...26, 36, 47
Power and the Glory, The...94
problematic individual...68
psychological novel...97

reader sympathy...42-43
Real Life of Alejandro Mayta, The...97, 132
realism...5-12
   imported...83
   in Spain...104
Red and the Black, The...90

Reeve, Clara
    on novel versus romance...18
Remembrance of Things Past...97
Richardson, Dorothy...81
Richardson, Samuel...80-81
Robbe-Grillet, Alain
    on the novel of characters...131
Robinson Crusoe...32, 37, 40, 66
Rojas, Fernando de...104
Roland...21
romance...130-131
romance versus epic...21
Rulfo, Juan...26

Sánchez Ferlioso, Rafael...73
Sacchario...121
Sarduy, Severo...110
Sarmiento, Domingo Faustino...23
Sarraute, Nathalie
    on character...92
satire...130
Scholes, Robert
    fabulation...130
    on novel versus fabulation...26
Scholes, Robert and Robert Kellogg
    on character...19
    on character and author...82
    on conflict...10, 12, 80
    on individual and society...63
    on mimetic characterization...101
    on novel versus romance...21
    on romance...131
    on romance versus picaresque...25
    on types of characterization...45
    on values...14
Schorer, Mark
    on conflict in the novel...86
Scott, Sir Walter...17
Seltzer, Alvin J....39
    on reality...125
    on types of conflict...40
Simms, William Gilmore

    on novel versus romance...18-19
Slonim, Marc
    on Russian literature...109
socialist realism...93, 112
society...4, 12
Solzhenitsyn, Alexander...122-123
    on the individual and conflict...87
Spain
    and dissent...105-106
    realism...104
Spanish American fiction...83
    the Boom...83-84, 112
    versus Brazilian...85
Spearman, Diana
    on novel as genre...28-29
Stendahl...83, 95
structure
    and authorial interference...56
    and individuation...57
    and mimesis...56-57
subjective novel...97
Swingewood, Alan
    on character and conflict...96
    on dual nature of the novel...89-90
    on individualism and socialism...73
    on literature under Stalin...121
    on novel and socialism...74
    on Solzhenitsyn...123
    on Utopia and the novel...39

Terra Nostra...132
Thackaray, W.M....98
Three Trapped Tigers...98
Tillyard, E.M.W....110
time...8
    chronos...9, 21, 42
    kairos...9, 21
Time of the Hero, The...132
Todorov, Tzvetan...18, 25
    on character...14
    on genre...4

on genres and social history...22
on verisimilitude...6
Tolstoy, Leo...50-51, 55, 97
   as dissident...94
   on art and social message...49
   on novel and social message...94
Tom Jones...34, 43-44, 48-49
Trachtenberg, Allen
   on novelists and uncertainty...100
Tres tristes tigres...98
Tristram Shandy...98
Trollope, Anthony...34, 81-82, 98
   on characters and authors...35
Trotsky, Leon
   on art and the revolution...118-119
   on individualism and socialism...73
Turnell, Martin
   on naturalism and the novel...99
   on structure...57

Ultima mujer y el próximo combate, La...121
Ulysses...47, 97-98
Una familia lejana...132
Unamuno, Miguel de...98

Vanity Fair...44-45
Vargas Llosa, Mario...20, 129, 132
   and the problem of verisimilitude...8
   on novel as deicide...91, 94
   on rebellion of novelist...92
verisimilitude...10
Vicens Vives, Jaime
   on Cervantes...106

War and Peace...33, 36, 44, 46, 50, 55
Ward, Wilfrid P....53

Watt, Ian...34, 68
   on character and conflict...41
   on character and reader...54
   on character and setting...37
   on character versus plot...11-12
   on epistolary novel...82
   on individualism and the novel...64-65, 79
   on novel in England...67
   on realism...8
   on women and the novel...81
West, Paul...107
Williams, Raymond...62, 127
   on art and socialism...116
   on conflict in the novel...71
   on genre theory...27
   on heroism...76
   on individual/social relationships...43, 59-60
   on individualism and proletariat...74
   on novel and industrialization...84
   on novel and middle class...68
   on novel as genre...x
   on novel in England...67
   on realism...70
   on realist tradition...42, 44
   on women and the Industrial Revolution...81
women
   and history of the novel...81
   and Industrial Revolution...81
   and novel...82
Woolf, Virginia
   on character and novel...31-32
   on character and society...40
Wright, Austin M....29-30
   on novel as genre...1-2

Zola, Emile...99